PERFORMING BACH'S VOCAL MUSIC

by

PAUL STEINITZ

Addington Press
RSCM/Mowbray

This Edition exclusively licensed by the
Royal School of Church Music to Hinshaw Music, Inc.
P.O. Box 470, Chapel Hill, NC 27514
Sole Selling Agent

First published in 1980
by Addington Press, Addington Palace,
Croydon, CR9 5AD

ISBN 0 906851 04 1

Typeset by Lowe & Brydone Printers Limited, Thetford, Norfolk
and printed in Great Britain by
David Green Printers Ltd., Kettering, Northamptonshire

DEDICATION

To members of the London Bach Society who, over a period of some thirty
years, have shared with me the unique experience of studying and performing
nearly all the vocal works of Bach.

PERFORMING BACH'S
VOCAL MUSIC

By the same author:

Bach's Passions (published by Elek)
German Choral Music 1630–1750
(Volume 5 of *The New Oxford History of Music*)
Harmony in Context (with Stella Sterman, published by
  Belwin-Mills)

FOREWORD

by
Sir Adrian Boult

It is indeed good news that The Royal School of Church Music has combined with Mowbray to issue a new series of guides to the standard choral works. It is equally good to know that the first of these will be devoted to J. S. Bach, and is in the hands of Dr. Paul Steinitz who has done such splendid work since 1946 when he formed the London Bach Society, and later, when he took over the music of St. Bartholomew the Great, Smithfield and has earned the gratitude of all Bach lovers ever since.

Dr. Steinitz has chosen a splendid series of chapter headings, and it is hoped that the other books in the series will be similarly planned. There will be detailed information about almost every possible aspect of the performance of Bach's masterpieces. The character of the music and how to approach its interpretation with large forces or small, with modern instruments or, if available, with special instruments of the period and a note about eighteenth century practice, the manner of balancing and rehearsing soloists, choir and orchestra and even on the availability of the performing material where this presents problems.

There are very few books with this kind of detail, particularly of the music which nowadays offer so many different styles of treatment. It will be a great help to many of us to get this information into some kind of perspective, and the freedom of choice will be a great help to all choral conductors.

I very much hope that this series will gradually cover many different types of choral music, and if experts like Dr. Steinitz are responsible for them, they will be much welcomed by all concerned.

PREFACE

This book is primarily intended to help people who do not have much expertise. I am thinking particularly of those that work outside the larger centres of musical activity.

ACKNOWLEDGEMENTS

I am indebted to Professor Ivor Keys and Dr. Lionel Dakers for helpful advice about the plan and content of this book, and to my wife for constant support during the writing of it and for typing the first draft.

CONTENTS

INTRODUCTION

The number of performances in Britain of Bach's vocal works has been increasing in recent years. In London the Passions are now so popular that they are often crowded out of the season to which they properly belong and are given during the post- instead of pre-Easter period and in festivals at any place and any time. The Christmas Oratorio has also gained ground with the public recently. Most important of all, a greater number of church cantatas – there are nearly two hundred of them – is now to be heard from groups both large and small up and down the country, whereas in the mid-sixties, apart from half-a-dozen well-known ones, performances of them were still rare. In the fifties they were practically unknown to all except connoisseurs.

The result of this upsurge of interest in Bach's vocal works is that the numerous problems which arise in performing them have now become a subject of great importance to a vast number of musicians. Until recently these problems concerned only a few specialist performers; most conductors and singers were content to ignore all but a few well-known works and to present these without paying too much attention to style. Today stylistic Bach is no longer reserved for specialist groups; nearly everyone realises that Bach's music is totally unlike that which has been composed since his death and that it cannot properly be performed in a later style. Even small unambitious groups now want to present it as 'correctly' as possible, knowing that the music will be more effective that way, and its meaning will make a better impact on an audience.

The problems are not only musical ones. One of the biggest obstacles encountered in presenting anything other than the major works is acquiring the material, and acquiring it at a reasonable price. The answers to the purely musicological problems, namely those connected with 'performance practice' can be found in various corners of various books and in articles, but these are not easy for the non-specialist person to track down, and, in any case, all the answers would not be found in one source. In short, the constant enquiries one receives by letter, telephone and through chance encounter about how to do or obtain this or that work or how to perform some particular passage, have made it plain that there is now an urgent need for a 'Performing Bach' guide book.

Not that anyone has all the answers, nor will they, nor could they be presented here; indeed, it would be boring if a fairly wide area of performance practice was not left for experimentation. I have ranged widely through Bach's vocal compositions in professional public performances (in semi-private ones it is possible to skate over some problems) for about a quarter of a century and some of what has been learned forms the basis of this book.

I have thought it best to make the order of chapters match the order in which the arrangements for performances would, or should, be made. The word 'should' is used advisedly, for readers may be astonished to learn that one can get telephone calls quite often, not just occasionally, from people who have a performance coming up in two or three weeks' time asking how on earth they can get hold of the music! 'Music' may mean orchestral parts, which *are* hard to come by, or vocal scores, or even a full score for the conductor! In Chapter 1, when dealing with the Passions, the old numbering (i.e. that of the *Bachgesellschaft* and Schmieder's catalogue) is used, but the new numbering of the *Neue Bach Ausgabe* is shown in brackets.

REPERTOIRE

With the music of most baroque composers the pieces one might have as first choices for performances are not always the best from a practical point of view. That is to say, the acquisition of the performing materials may be difficult, as already mentioned, or the resources required – soloists, instruments, and so on – may be such that if due care is not exercised, fees may have to be paid to singers or players whose roles, though musically very important, are otherwise very small. The first of these points is dealt with in Chapter 2, but discussion of the second one belongs here, for there must be very few, if any, musical directors or promoters who have unlimited financial resources behind them, and who do not have to plan things as far as possible so that not only is the music taken care of, but unnecessary extravagance is also avoided.

The essence of baroque instrumentation being variety between the movements, whereas in the post-baroque era basically variety is found *within* each movement, it follows that planning programmes and rehearsals can be a difficult and financially hazardous operation. Detailed reasons for this are as follows: firstly, the orchestration of each work may be different; secondly, all the instruments will not be playing all the time in any one work; thirdly, one instrument or solo voice may appear once in a work and not in any of the other works one might at first wish to choose. Thus, viewed entirely from the economic and not the musical standpoint, a good deal of money can be laid out with very little return. To give a few examples:

(i) Cantata No. 90 requires a trumpet which plays a splendid *obbligato* in only one piece, the bass aria No. 3; it might also double the soprano line in the final chorale, but no instrumentation is given for this movement.

(ii) In cantata No. 135 a trombone is called for to add colour to the continuo line, which is the *cantus firmus*, but only in the opening chorus; a cornett is also scored for only in the final plain chorale and just to double the soprano melody.

(iii) Cantata No. 171 calls for a solo bass, but he only sings a *secco* recitative and arioso; it also calls for an alto soloist, who only sings one *secco* recitative.

(iv) If Parts I–III of the Christmas Oratorio are performed as one concert, the solo soprano will only have one – very important – recitative (in Part II) and a part in a duet (in Part III), a movement which, although charming, by tradition is often omitted.

These situations are not unusual, but very common, because, broadly speaking, Bach had his instrumentalists and solo singers (concertists from the choir) on call all the time. This is a slight over-simplification of the facts, but is valid for the purposes of the argument. Therefore it is obvious that programme planning must be such that the orchestral and solo vocal resources of the various works in any one concert coincide as much as possible, if costs are to be kept to a reasonable level.

With these considerations in mind we can now give thought to the discussion of repertoire from the point of view of the music and its suitability for various occasions and situations.

(a) **Passions**

Basically the choice is between the St John and the St Matthew Passions (BWV 245 and 244 respectively), although a reconstruction of the mostly lost St Mark Passion has been published[1]. The St Luke Passion, although printed in the *Bachgesellschaft*, is not by J. S. Bach, and so does not come into our discussion. The new full score of the St John[2] includes in an appendix the different versions of the work which Bach used for his second, third and fourth performances; at least the second version (1725) is musically interesting enough to merit occasional hearings.

The exact resources required for each movement of the Passions as well as for every other Bach work are listed in Schmieder's Thematic Catalogue[3]. This is to be found in all University and most Music College libraries and in the larger municipal libraries. As, however, the Passions are probably

4

the works most often performed, it will be convenient for the reader if a list of what they require is given here.*

St John Passion. Orchestra: Bach calls for two flutes, two oboes, both doubling *oboes da caccia* (modern cor anglais), and one doubling *oboe d'amore*, one bassoon, one lute, two *viole d'amore*, one *viola da gamba*, strings and organ. Voices: six soloists (or four – see below), namely, an Evangelist (tenor), Jesus (bass), and, for arias and smaller character parts, one each of soprano, alto or contralto, tenor and bass. These would have been the concertists in Bach's choir. It is possible to omit the doubling of *oboe d'amore* by the second oboe as this is employed simply to cover the few low notes beyond the compass of the ordinary oboe in one or two choruses, and these are played by second violins.

It is more important to have the *viole d'amore* and if possible the lute (but see below) because of their special tone qualities, for these impart such an exquisite colour to the numbers in which they are involved. If one were to cut both 31 and 32 (19 and 20) it would greatly damage the shape of the work as regards balance between narration, interpolation and chorale; omitting the first of them, number 31 (19), would be a grievous musical loss and as far as cost is concerned not entirely necessary, for the new score gives authority for organ or harpsichord (octave higher) as lute substitutes and muted solo violins as replacements of the *viole d'amore*. This leaves only the *viola da gamba* as an instrument which may be difficult to obtain in more remote areas. Again, its tone colour is unique, and in this case no other instument can replace it and produce a comparable sound; the part is often played on a 'cello' in the absence of a *gamba*, but the effect is not only entirely different, it is usually clumsy. It can be said though, that at the time of writing the number of *gamba* players is increasing almost daily, and an enquiry from one of the many early music groups could produce positive results. Regarding soloists, in Germany sometimes one tenor and one bass respectively sing all the tenor and bass roles, but this is not a practice to be recommended, not only because the strain on the voices is too great, but also because the

*A breakdown of the resources needed for each movement of both Passions, with a commentary, is given in P. Steinitz: *Bach's Passions*, London, 1979.

dramatic effect suffers, at any rate in public as opposed to recorded or broadcast performances.

The requirements of the St Matthew Passion are as follows: two orchestras, each consisting of two flutes, two oboes, one bassoon*, strings and organ. In orchestra I a *viola da gamba* in numbers 65 and 66 (56 and 57) and two recorders in number 25 (19) are also needed.[4]

Some oboes have to double on other instruments, but this is explained below. In regard to voices, two four-part (S.A.T.B.) choruses, and strictly speaking, ten solo singers; but in modern practice only six (see below) are required. These are: an Evangelist (tenor), Jesus (bass), and, for arias, accompanied recitatives and smaller character parts, ideally two each of soprano, alto, tenor and bass, one from each choir, but in practice today their parts are taken by only four singers, one of each voice. As in St John, originally these would have been the concertists; the solo work is fairly evenly divided between the two choirs, though most of the small parts belong to choir I. The first and second orchestras accompany the first and second choirs and the soloists drawn from them respectively. In addition, a *ripieno* choir is needed to sing a chorale (independent) in number 1 and to double the *tutti* sopranos in number 35 (29). The method employed above of listing the oboes is in order to avoid confusion. In fact, although strictly speaking only two *players* are needed at any one time in orchestra I, there are *obbligato* parts also in this orchestra for two *oboes d'amore* and two *oboes da caccia* (played by cor anglais, but in future referred to as *oboes da caccia*). In orchestra II there are parts for two *oboes d'amore* but only in the chorus number 35 (29), and these double the *oboes d'amore* of orchestra I.† It is not possible today for the oboists in orchestra I to double *da caccias* AND *d'amores*; the changes of instrument involve too much strain, and in any case number 26 (20) with solo oboe must follow number 25 (19) with two *da caccias* immediately. So, in order to avoid excessive and unnecessary expense,

---

*By implication and musical demand; it is not formally listed.

†If the oboes of orchestra II only double on *da caccias* then in number 35 (29) two *d'amores* from orchestra I and two ordinary oboes from orchestra II will be doubling each other. Which would be a pity, but not a calamity.

what can happen in practice, and usually does, is that the oboes of orchestra I double only on *d'amores*, and the oboes of orchestra II double only on *da caccias* (but see below). In number 70 (60) there are parts for *oboes da caccia* (which properly belong to orchestra I) *and* for the oboes of orchestra II. If, as suggested above, the oboes of orchestra II are playing *da caccias* in this number, the oboes of orchestra I, who are silent in this movement could play these small parts, but they would have to have the necessary music inserted into their scores. However, this is a very small role, and the strings of orchestra II double it; the oboe sound certainly gives an edge to the choir II interpolations which it doubles, but it could be omitted if the time for preparation and rehearsal of it were not available.

All this simply means that:

(i)   Orchestra I: oboes double *oboes d'amore*. The parts in orchestra I for *da caccias* found in their music need to be deleted, copied and transferred to the music for the oboes of orchestra II. The music of number 70 (60) for the oboes of orchestra II needs to be transferred to the music of the oboes of orchestra I.

(ii) Orchestra II: oboes double on *oboes da caccias* and if possible, in number 35 (29) only, on *oboes d'amore*.

If six oboes are available, two of them will play *da caccias* and will need the *da caccia* music of orchestra I.

As will be seen from the above list, the St Matthew Passion calls for only one 'obsolete' instrument, namely the *viola da gamba*; recorders are hardly obsolete, but they could be replaced by flutes in number 25 (19) without too much damage to the tone picture; the remarks made about the *viola da gamba* in the section about St John apply here. The duration of the St John Passion is about two hours ten minutes, and of the St Matthew Passion three hours twenty-five minutes.

Regarding cuts, it should not be necessary to omit any section of the St John in normal circumstances. But if necessity calls, then number 32 (20) and *one* of the arias in the second part which are in or near the death scene, that is 58, 60 or 63 (30, 32 or 35), could be cut without too great structural damage or disturbance of key scheme being

7

incurred. Omitting number 58 (30) would mean that one would miss Bach's wonderful transformation of the final phrase of 57 (29), 'It is finished', into the main theme of 58 (30). Likewise 62 (34) transfers the shudders of the earth in the previous recitative to the heart in the arioso. Comparable losses occur by cutting 60 or 63 (32 or 35) of course. Part I has only three arias, but, although the first two tend to hold up the action, it would seriously upset the shape of Part I not to have both of them performed; moreover, the important thematic connection between numbers 12 (8) and 13 (9) would be lost; if one of these two arias must go, the preference therefore is for 11 (7). A purist might omit numbers 18 (12c) (the last eight bars) and 61 (33) because the texts of both are borrowed from St Matthew's gospel; but 18 (12c), Peter's weeping, is inseparable from 19 (13) which, in a sense is his aria, so that cutting it could mean losing this as well. The only recitatives not completely essential to the central Passion story are 64 (36) and 66 (38). If either of these were omitted then possibly the chorale 65 (37) could be cut too. One piece that should never be omitted is the chorale number 40 (22), for it is the centre point of the palindrome in Part II[5].

Cutting parts of the St Matthew Passion has some practical justification because of the work's great length. But in considering what to omit it should always be borne in mind that Bach's overall plan is masterly in its arrangements of contrasts of keys, instrumental and vocal colour, moments of high emotional tension and moments of relaxation, and the employment of very small groups and very large groups of performers.

Various cuts are suggested in the Novello Elgar-Atkins edition. Some of these are of *da capos* where playing only the opening *ritornello* is suggested after the second section. There is a case for omitting the second section *and* the *da capos* of arias if cuts are necessary; this preserves a better balance of keys. Other cuts indicated in the Novello edition are worth considering, but the omission of the arias 61 (52) *and* 66 (57) with its preceding accompanied recitative 65 (56) would remove all the moments of repose so well planned for this section of the work. Other possible cuts, but certainly not more than one or two of them in any one performance, are

40 (34), 48 (40), 51 (42) and 58 (49). Although the chorale fantasia number 35 (29) is one of the finest pieces ever composed, it is worth mentioning that Bach in his first performance of the work simply had the plain chorale *Jesum lass ich nicht von mir*, BWV 244b, to close Part I. It is also possible to cut small parts of the narration if due care is exercised in preserving a convincing tonal structure. The indications of standing and sitting for the choirs which are given in the Elgar-Atkins Novello edition, sometimes in the middle of a movement, can disturb the continuity of a dramatic recitative. This matter should certainly be re-thought very carefully.

(b) Oratorios

There are only three oratorios to consider, for Christmas, BWV 248, Easter, BWV 249, and Ascension, BWV 11. The feature which distinguishes them from the cantatas is that each has a 'story' running through it, though in his final version of the Easter Oratorio Bach eliminated all the *named* characters while preserving much of their original music; moreover the story is only present by implication.

The Christmas Oratorio consists of six cantatas, one each for the first three days of Christmas, New Year's Day (Circumcision), the Sunday after New Year's Day and Epiphany. The choruses and arias are parodies of music which Bach composed a year earlier to secular texts, and the work therefore suffered from criticism by Schweitzer and other earlier scholars who did not understand that there was nothing inherently wrong in transferring music from one text to another. If two movements have basically the same mood or affection the music transfers easily. A common example of this is when the music set originally to words in praise of an earthly king is put to words in praise of the heavenly King, for example, when the first movement of *Preise dein Glucke*, BWV 215, becomes *Osanna in excelsis* in the Mass in B minor. It is interesting, however, that transfers do not seem to have been made in the other direction, that is from sacred to secular texts. In recent years the Christmas Oratorio has gained much more of the popularity which it deserves. In fact, hardly any movements can be singled out as falling below a high standard. As performances spread out over six days, or even two or more days, are usually economically impossible, one has to decide what to cut if the total of approximately two and a half hours' music is too much for one concert, and cannot be properly rehearsed in the time which may be available. The simplest and musically most satisfactory thing is to perform only so many *whole cantatas*; but there may be reasons for more haphazard cuts. So few numbers in Parts I and II are excessively long and all are such superb pieces that cutting any of them is to be avoided if possible. If not possible, then one could consider omitting the *da capo* and/or middle part of number 5 or number 19.

In Part III, either number 29 or 31 could be dropped, as between them they do rather hold up the unfolding of the story. To cut both would mean that Part III would lose all the substantial movements between the first two choruses (24 and 26) and the final chorale. In Part IV one could cut – albeit sadly – the tenor aria 41, and, if only one tenor is used, this would save vocal strain for the Evangelist. In Parts V and VI, although some arias and ensembles are on the long side, only one in each part should be cut if structural balance is to be preserved. In any case, to cut both the soprano and tenor arias in Part VI would place too much strain on the first trumpet, who has a very florid *obbligato* in the closing chorale as well as an exacting part in the long opening chorus, and a reasonable break between these two is essential. On the other hand, it is possible to telescope Parts V and VI so that a reasonably complete, if lop-sided 'cantata' results if numbers 48–51, 61 and 62 are omitted. But the only excuse for such action would be to ensure that the biggest and most effective concerted movements and the recitatives that complete the story are not lost even when one is working to a strict time limit.

The Easter Oratorio, like the Christmas Oratorio, is mostly a parody of earlier music[6]. It begins with a Sinfonia in two movements; the first is an exhilarating one with trumpets and timpani in D major and the second, in B minor, is expressive, but here the alignment of rhythms needs some thought (see below Chapter 3a). The Sinfonia is followed by a long opening chorus, also very stirring and also in D, which makes forty full score pages of triple time all in D major; however, they are separated by four *minutes* of contrast in B minor, although still with the same key signature. On balance, the splendour of the music justifies this*. Several later numbers are exceptionally beautiful, and the work should certainly be heard more often.

Like the Christmas Oratorio, the Ascension Oratorio which is printed in the BG in a cantata volume, has an Evangelist, but here there are no definite characters. However, 'two men in white garments' appear, into whose mouths the Evangelist puts words. The opening and closing movements rank as two of Bach's very finest creations, and he himself evidently thought well of the alto aria No. 4, for he used it later as the basis of the *Agnus Dei* in the Mass in B minor.

(c) Masses

The Mass in B minor BWV 232, like the Passions, needs no advocate; it must be the most popular Bach work for all those who have the resources with which to perform it. The demands which it makes technically are very great and are too often underestimated. It is frustrating that the economics of presenting this Mass in public are nearly always such as to necessitate a performance in one 'sitting' (though with the statutory short interval of course), for there are disadvantages in compressing the work in this way. Bach compiled it − partly from earlier compositions − rather with the purpose of offering the very best of his art in a complete setting of the Mass than of creating a work for practical use, and it is very doubtful if he ever envisaged a performance of it complete at any one time; the idea of presenting the work as a public concert would hardly have entered his head. This explains the monotony of scoring and key in the section from *Et vitam venturi* to the first *Osanna* a section which is therefore a severe strain on both voices and trumpets if performed without an interval before the *Sanctus*. If one adds

---

*It may be contended that Bach risked monotony of key and of orchestral colour also in the Mass in B minor (cf Ic).

Confiteor and *Benedictus* (with the second *Osanna*) which respectively precede and follow this section, one has seven movements following each other all with the same or closely related key signatures and largely the same orchestration. Therefore there is a strong case for having two full intervals, one before and one after the *Credo*, or, at worst, one long and one short interval, when giving the work in public.

The four Lutheran Masses, BWV 233, 234, 235 and 236. have been neglected in the past, because, like BWV 248 and 249, they are largely parodies of cantatas. Although in a few cases, for example the first movement of the Mass in G minor, the parody is not entirely successful, in general the transcriptions work well, and these works can be strongly recommended. The playing time of each is about half an hour, the chorus has rather more to do than in the average cantata, and the orchestral resources are not extravagant. Except in the first Mass (which is arguably the best and includes two horns) only two upper woodwind instruments plus (optional) bassoon are called for in any one work. These Masses include transcriptions of some of the finest movements from the cantatas.

Before leaving the subject of Masses, two single Mass movements are worth mentioning. The first is the *Kyrie eleison*, BWV 233a, a version by the composer for S.S.A.T.B. chorus and continuo of the corresponding movement from the Mass in F; it is a short, very expressive movement which includes the chorale *Christe, Lamm Gottes* (the *Agnus Dei*)[7], and is inexpensive to perform. The second is the *Sanctus in D*, BWV 238[8], a short, cheerful piece for four-part chorus with an independent first violin part; the other instruments, *cornetto* (could be oboe), violin II, viola and continuo double the voices.

(d) Magnificats

Bach composed two versions of the Latin Magnificat, the first in E flat and the second in D, both numbered BWV 243 in Schmieder's catalogue. Apart from these, the text of Cantata 10 is a free paraphrase in German of the Magnificat which uses the plainsong *tonus perigrinus* associated with the hymn as a *cantus firmus* in three movements, one of which is a beautiful duet for alto and tenor, *Et misericordia*. Bach himself must have liked this movement well, for he later transcribed it as one of his six Schübler organ preludes. Cantata 10 makes a fine and very interesting item in any one programme devoted to Magnificats.

The E flat Magnificat is simply an earlier version of the well known work in D. The scoring is slightly different; for example it uses recorders instead of flutes. It also contains four delightful Christmas interludes, and the publishers of the new Bach edition in their orchestral material of the more popular D major work have wisely seen fit to include the last three of them, transposed down so that they can be used with the version in D. The first interlude is an *a capella* type of chorus, which also needs a *basso continuo* part; this has therefore to be written out because a totally unaccompanied piece of Bach would not sound right somehow,* especially when surrounded by accompanied movements. Both the E flat and D major Magnificats use the plainsong *cantus firmus*, though scored differently, in *Suscepit Israel*. Between the two versions there are also minor differences in notes and word underlay.

(e) Church cantatas

As stated in the Introduction, more cantatas are now heard than was the case a decade or two ago; nevertheless they are still to a great extent unexplored, and for reasons that are not hard to find or understand. Organisations most likely to promote them are choral societies and church choirs, and naturally they look for works in which choral singing plays the largest part. In the cantatas this is not generally the case, comparatively few having more than one chorus and some 'solo' cantatas having none, not even a chorale; moreover most cantatas call for several soloists, and all need an orchestra. If ways round these 'drawbacks' can be found and the cantatas can become part of the standard repertory, the rewards will be found to be great indeed. Few today would deny that a great deal of Bach's finest music at present lies buried in the cantatas. Certainly this is the unanimous opinion

*But I admit that this is a matter of opinion.

of all who have had the chance to explore them thoroughly.

Some of the obstacles to performance can vanish if one is not too puristically minded over making simple compromises. For example, a number of arias and *ariosos* can be treated chorally or semi-chorally with reasonably good effect. And while it would be very wrong not to employ professional soloists whenever possible, choral or semi-choral treatment is to be preferred to an inexperienced or weak amateur singer, or to not giving the work a hearing at all. All arias that consist simply of unembellished chorale melodies are more effective chorally in any case.

In List A (see Appendix B), suggestions are given of arias in the cantatas which could be performed chorally or semi-chorally.

Recommending a complete list of cantatas suitable for all kinds of organisations, whose conditions and musical capabilities are very varied, would be a lengthy operation. List A may help to put some works within reach which would otherwise be out of it. List B (see Appendix B) may help too, for it gives all the cantatas which contain more than one chorus; to list the enormous number which have only one chorus and a chorale would take up too much space and would duplicate what already exists*, but those with a big chorus in two sections taking up a major portion of the whole work are included. Experience has convinced me that few, if any, of the cantatas can be written off as dull, although a few of them are uneven in quality; therefore a separate list of specially recommended ones is not included, but in List B some specially outstanding works are given a ★; this I admit is a questionable procedure and such value judgements must be regarded to some extent as the personal opinions of the author. However, those who are exploring the cantatas for the first time may find such guidance useful.

Finally, List C (see Appendix B) gives the solo cantatas, including those with a final chorale; this is to assist the process of elimination for those who are chiefly concerned with choral concerts. As in List B specially fine works are marked with a ★.

The term 'solo cantata' may mean works for a single solo

*In Schmieder's catalogue, for instance.

voice or for any number of soloists from one to four. Outstanding cantatas for a single voice are 51, 52, 56, 82, 169, 170 and 199. The outstanding ones which call for more than one solo voice are shown in List C; again, this is necessarily a personal opinion, but may be helpful to those who are inexperienced in selecting from such a vast number of works.

(f) Secular cantatas

These works, running roughly from BWV 198 to BWV 222, are divided into solo cantatas for one or more voices and cantatas involving chorus and soloists. As many of them were written for special festive occasions when resources would have been slightly larger than for a normal church service, we often find Bach calling for very large orchestras. For example, the magnificent Funeral Ode for Queen Eberhardine of Poland, BWV 198, is scored for two flutes, two oboes doubling *d'amores*, two lutes, two *gambas*, strings and harpsichord. BWV 201 is scored for a big orchestra with trumpets and drums, six soloists and chorus; BWV 205 calls for a full Bach orchestra including three trumpets and, in addition, two horns, *viola d'amore* and *viola da gamba*, with four soloists and chorus. The normal keyboard continuo instrument for these secular cantatas would have been harpsichord. It must be said that nearly all the secular cantatas, which include the many secular forerunners of favourite church works (for details see Schmieder's catalogue)[9], are quite magnificent works and absolutely demand more public performances than they get at present. The texts are sometimes just fulsome praise of some – to us – unimportant regal or municipal personages, but are certainly no worse than some texts set by such seventeenth and eighteenth century composers as Purcell or Boyce. Exceptionally fine choral works are BWV numbers 213 and 214 (both used in the Christmas Oratorio), and 207, which magnificently utilizes movements from Brandenburg Concerto No. 1. But to pick these out is really unfair on the others. Of the solo ones, 202 (Wedding), 211 (Coffee), and 212 (Peasant) are already justly famous, and 210 (Wedding) is equally good.

(g) **Motets and hymns**

The six motets BWV 225 to BWV 230 are so well known that they only need mention here for the sake of making this chapter complete. There is a very strong case for performing the motets with doubling orchestral instruments, seeing that an autographed instrumental version (BWV 226a) exists in which violin I, violin II, viola and cello double chorus I, oboe I, oboe II, *oboe da caccia* (or cor anglais) and bassoon double chorus II and organ and *violone* (or double bass) have a composite part in *Der Geist hilft unserer Schwachheit auf* *. About a century ago Spitta pointed out the instrumental quality of the vocal writing of these works and doubling certainly aids articulation; it therefore helps to clarify textures, though more so in some works than in others[10]. To ensure a correct bass line and grammatical eighteenth century harmony, the motets must, as a minimum, have a sixteen foot preferably string (though organ pedals would do) *basso continuo*, that is, sounding an octave below the bass vocal line, and organ supplying the harmonies above it. *Sei Lob und Preis* BWV 231, for S.A.T.B. and doubling instruments, included in the Peters edition of the motets, though not comparable in magnificence to those for double choir, is a vigorous, cheerful little work, lasting about four minutes, which can make a good opening or closing to a concert of miscellaneous items.

Finally, there are sixty-nine melodies that Bach collected (he *composed* very few of them) and to which he supplied figured basses for Schemelli's hymn book.† These make admirable anthems for church use and can also fill in gaps in a miscellaneous programme. These hymns have suffered various sets of realisations of the figured basses over the years, but very few have been accurate. A list of these versions is given, with the melodies and figured basses themselves, in Riemanschneider's collection of the three hundred and seventy-one chorales published by Schirmer.

---

*In applying this type of scoring to other motets it is necessary to have a composite continuo (violone or double bass) at sixteen foot pitch created by writing out the 'real' bass line throughout. One or two publishers have now begun to issue instrumental parts for the motets.
†BWV 439–507.

The Royal School of Church Music has recently published a few also in English and German[11]. Wüllner's realisations have commendable points, and there is a clean, but unrealised and untranslated edition issued by Peters.

2

PERFORMING MATERIAL
AND HOW TO OBTAIN IT

(a) **Vocal scores**

Obtaining vocal material can present problems, but these are mostly financial: in other words, it is not that material is unavailable, but that the price of it in the United Kingdom can be very high under present economic conditions. This is not the fault of publishers who, because Bach's music is German and not English, are mostly German. They have to contend with such matters as unfavourable exchange rates and the fact that there is a comparatively small demand for Bach's lesser known works in Britain. First then, to describe as accurately as possible a changing situation regarding the availability of material as it exists at the time of writing. This will be done under the heading of vocal and chorus scores, orchestral parts (including keyboard continuo), and full scores, and will follow the order of classification of works as in Chapter 1. Information is tabulated in cases where it makes for clearer presentation; it is compiled from publishers' current (1979) catalogues, but readers should of course not expect its reliability to last very long.

The prices of the works shown in the tables vary according to the country of origin, those from Germany being the most expensive. Miniature scores are comparatively cheap and indeed tend to be the most economical kind of vocal score. For choirs, the cheapest of all is a 'choruses only' edition, especially if it is hireable, but these are mostly only in German.

As tables A, B and C give information about all the major works, we will now consider the cantatas, both secular and sacred.

Vocal scores of all cantatas have been published by BREITKOPF with German texts; some also have English (singable) versions.

PETERS have issued quite a large number in German only.

NOVELLO have thirty-six, in English only. They are given in Appendix B, List D.

Availability of Passions

	Vocal scores			Chorus pts		Orch: Pts inc. kb		Full scores	Comments
	Hire	*Buy*	*Borrow*	*Hire*	*Buy*	*Hire*	*Buy*		
St Matthew Passion	Bärenreiter small quantity for soli only	Bärenreiter German and English	–	BV	BV	BV	BV	Bärenreiter: large and miniature	This is the new NBA authoritative score in German only (see below for wording).
		Breitkopf & Härtel	–	–	B & H	–	B & H	B & H	German only
	Mills (in future)	Mills	–	–	–	Mills (in future)	Mills	Mills: BG edition large and small	
		Eulenberg	–	–	–	–	–	Eulenberg miniature score BG edition	German only
	Novello	Novello	Novello from libraries	–	–	Novello	–	Novello: BG edition	Vocal material in English only
	Peters: if large enough quantities	Peters	–	–	–	Peters	Peters	Peters	German only
St John Passion	BV: small amounts for soli	BV	–	BV	BV	BV	BV	BV large and small	This is the newest and most authentic score available (NBA) German
		B & H	–	–	B & H	–	B & H?	B & H	
		Eulenberg min. score	–	–	–	–	–	Eulenberg min. score	German only

Availability of Passions

	Vocal scores			Chorus pts		Orch: Pts inc. kb		Full scores	Comments
	Hire	*Buy*	*Borrow*	*Hire*	*Buy*	*Hire*	*Buy*		
St John Passion (cont.)	Mills	Mills	–	–	–	Mills	Mills	Mills: BG edition large and small	Vocal material in English only
	Novello	Novello	Novello from libraries	–	–	Novello	Novello	Novello: BG edition	German only
	Peters: if large amts	Peters	–	–	–	Peters	Peters	Peters	Ed. Mendel: German, and singable, though not very good English
	–	Schirmer	–	–	–	–	–	–	
St Mark Passion	–	Hänssler reconstruction	–	–	–	Hänssler	Hänssler	Hänssler	German only

Availability of Oratorios

	Vocal scores			Chorus Pts		Orch: pts inc. kb		Full scores	Comments
	Hire	*Buy*	*Borrow*	*Hire*	*Buy*	*Hire*	*Buy*		
Christmas Oratorio	BV probably only small amts for soli	BV	Some libraries	BV	BV	BV	BV	BV: large and small	This is the newest and most authoritative score (NBA)
		B & H	–	–	B & H	–	B & H	B & H: BG edition	German only
		Eulenberg	–	–	–	–	–	Eulenberg min. score BG edition	German only

20

	Vocal scores		Chorus Pts		Orch: pts inc. kb		Full scores	Comments
	Mills	Mills	—	—	Mills	Mills	Mills: BG edition large and min.	
	Novello	Novello	Novello: libraries	—	—	—	Novello: BG edition or Peters edition (on hire)	
	Peters if large amts	Peters	—	—	Peters	Peters	Peters	German only
Easter Oratorio		BV (eventually)			BV (eventually)		Bärenreiter	This is the newest and most authoritative score (NBA)
	B & H? (enquire)	B & H			B & H? (enquire)		Possibly B & H (hire) (enquire)	German only
		Hänssler				Hänssler	Hänssler	
	Mills (in future)	Mills			Mills (in future)	Mills	Mills	English
		Schott	Schott	Schott	Schott		Schott	German and English
Ascension Oratorio Cantata 11		BV (eventually)			BV	BV	Bärenreiter	This is the most authoritative NBA score.
	B & H?	B & H		B & H	B & H		B & H (hire)	German only
		Eulenberg					Eulenberg min score	
	Mills	Mills			Mills	Mills	Mills: large and small.	
	Novello	Novello	Novello from large public libraries		Novello		Novello (hire)	Novello vocal material in English only

Availability of *Masses and Magnificats*

	Vocal scores			Chorus pts		Orch: pts inc. kb.		Full Scores	Comments
	Hire	*Buy*	*Borrow*	*Hire*	*Buy*	*Hire*	*Buy*		
Mass in B Minor	BV only small amts for soli	BV		BV	BV	BV	BV	BV	This is the most authoritative NBA.
		B & H Eulenberg min. score			B & H		B & H	Breitkopf & Härtel Eulenberg min. score	
	Mills (in future) Novello	Mills				Mills in future Novello	Mills	Mills: BG edition large and min. Novello	All scores other than BV need more careful checking with NBA for word underlay than most works.
	Peters if large amounts	Novello	Novello from libraries			Peters	Peters	Peters	
		Peters							
Lutheran Masses (a) All four of them	BV (eventually)	Mills		BV (eventually)		BV (eventually)		BV	This is the latest and most authoritative score NBA; published 1978; performing material unlikely to follow for some years.
	B & H? Mills			B & H?		Mills	Mills	Mills	

22

	Vocal scores			Chorus pts		Orch: Pts inc. kb		Full scores	Comments
	Hire	Buy	Borrow	Hire	Buy	Hire	Buy		
(b) separately Mass in F	B & H?	Peters / B & H				B & H?		B & H hire	
Mass No. 2 in A	B & H / Novello	B & H / Novello		B & H / Novello	B & H	B & H?		B & H hire / Novello hire	
Mass No. 3 / Mass No. 4	B & H?	B & H / Novello		B & H		B & H?		B & H hire	
Magnificat In E flat	BV?	BV min. score						BV with D major version; Large and min.	This is the newest and most authoritative NBA score
In D major	BV?	BV		BV	BV	BV	BV	BV with E flat version	This is the newest and most authoritative NBA score
	B & H?	B & H		B & H?	B & H	Possibly B & H (enquire)	–	(B & H BG ed.)	All scores other than BV need more careful checking with the NBA score for word underlay, etc., than most other works.
		Eulenberg	Novello in most libraries					Eulenberg min. score	
	Novello	Novello				Novello		Novello (hire)	
	Mills (in future)	Mills				Mills (in future)	Mills	Mills (BG ed.) large and min.	
	Peters if large amounts	Peters				Peters	Peters	Peters	

BV = Bärenreiter
B & H = Breitkopf and Härtel
NBA = Neue Bach Ausgabe (New Bach Edition)

BELWIN MILLS have obtained the right to issue vocal scores, in German and/or English, of other publishers, and photographic reductions of full scores of the old BG edition (see below re orchestral material), usable as vocal scores, though the S.A. and T. voices are in C clefs and the print is small. The vocal scores issued by Mills are so numerous that it is simpler to list those which they do NOT at present publish (see Appendix B, List E).

BÄRENREITER are slowly issuing vocal scores of the cantatas which have been already published in NBA volumes of full scores, but there is a very considerable time lag.

CURWEN (Faber Music) have numbers 10 and 78 in English and German[1].

EULENBERG (through Schott) publish sixty cantatas in miniature full score with voice parts in modern clefs; the language is German, but some have singable English as an inset as well. The numbers are given in Appendix B, List F.

HÄNSSLER OF STUTTGART publish thirty-two cantatas; they are given in Appendix B, List G.

BROUDE BROTHERS New York, publish some thirty cantatas in miniature score (slightly larger than Eulenberg and considerably larger than Mills) in German with singable English insets.

To try and give entirely reliable information in 1979 about relative prices of the above when these are constantly increasing would be foolish and misleading. Only very general guidance can be given. Novello and Belwin Mills vocal scores are, naturally, the least expensive to buy in the United Kingdom. Miniature full scores, used as vocal scores, although comparatively cheap, have the disadvantage of their small size. At the time of writing, Eulenberg miniature scores range from about £1.20 to £1.40 per cantata. The Mills (Kalmus) miniature scores can each contain two, three, or even four works and so can work out the cheapest of all, but they have the greatest number of practical disadvantages (see above). It is strictly illegal to photocopy printed vocal scores otherwise than making the odd copy for study purposes, or with the permission of the publishers if the works are in short supply or out of print or out of copyright. The more the law is broken in this respect the more will publishers' prices continue to rise and the musical community suffer.

But Bach's *notes* are not copyright, and if choirs are prepared to sing from manuscript copies, xeroxed, the cost can be very low indeed.★ So many cantatas have only one chorus and one chorale or at most two of each, that it is possible to get the choral section(s) of them on to anything from two to ten sides which, at present prices, can work out at from sixpence to thirty pence per copy, or less if run off in very large numbers. The disadvantages are obvious, the chief one being that with only the choral sections to hand, choir members find it more difficult to identify themselves with the work as a whole.

In choosing which edition of a work to use, the deciding factors may not only be availability and cost, but whether English or German is going to be sung. There would be a great deal to be said for advocating the use of English if more than a handful of good, faithful English versions existed of *any* Bach vocal work, and by faithful I mean those that respect Bach's 'word-interpretative' settings by retaining the same association of the principal words and music as in the original. Too often either the sense is altered or the point of some specially 'affective' harmony, interval or rhythm is lost because the word-order is altered. A well known instance of this is when the following unusually huge downward leap designed to convey vividly the meaning of the word :'death' goes for nothing in one of the standard English translations: see Fig. 1.

Fig. 1   **Bass Aria, Cantata 4**

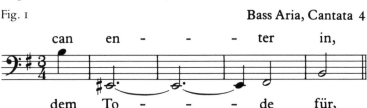

Admittedly, faithful translations are extremely difficult to achieve; those for the Evangelist's recitatives in the Passions are virtually impossible without substantially altering Bach's tunes rhythmically and melodically or adding many 'unnecessary' English words, as these tunes were only

★But manuscript copies should only be made from non-copyright material.

25

conceived to clothe the German text. The argument as to how important the tunes are and how important the English Bible (which version of it?) is, can be endless. To a lesser extent, because biblical and therefore sacrosanct words occur less frequently, the same sort of arguments apply to the cantatas.

It is better to perform Bach's masterpieces in bad English than not at all; better still to perform them in badly pronounced German, and best of all to perform them with good German pronunciation. There is no doubt that today provincial amateur choirs can sing quite well in German even if they find it difficult to believe this before trying. Most people are fairly good mimics, and so good patterning can be helpful in teaching the new language.* Apart from words and music association, the actual sound of German vowels and consonants enables the music to make a better impact than if it is wedded to sounds with which it had no original connection.

If German is used, then a literal English translation must be provided for the audience with at least headlines in German, better still, complete German and English texts. W. G. Whittaker's *The Cantatas of J. S. Bach*[2] provides word-by-word literal translations, albeit in impossible English, of every cantata. There are good translations by Derek McCulloch with many Archive records, and less reliable ones with the Das Alte Werk complete recordings; all these are copyright, and permission to use them must be requested.

In advocating the use of German whenever possible, I am not unmindful of its disadvantages, the chief of which is that singers have to make an effort to understand the meaning of it before their performances can be convincing. It is by no means impossible to make singable, faithful translations or to alter and adapt existing ones with reasonable success.

Before closing this section the point must be made – and its importance demands that it be repeated at other junctures in the book – that dynamics, phrasing and tempo marks given in nearly all vocal scores, other than those from Bärenreiter

---

*My own choir, the London Bach Society, has regular coaching from an ex-member who is a German.

and Curwen, should be viewed with the utmost suspicion and checked against urtext full scores and musical common sense.

(b) Orchestral material and full scores

The problems here are greater than in the case of vocal scores. Tables A, B and C give information about the major works; difficulties begin with the cantatas, but these difficulties are not so much due to the unavailability of the material as to the ignorance of musical directors concerning its whereabouts. Another snag is the out-of-date and over-edited nature of some of the orchestral parts which are available on hire and also still for purchase; such material is now confined in the main to German publications of some fifty years ago. Breitkopf and Härtel have in recent years produced some clean, *almost* entirely unedited parts, and Bärenreiter's orchestral material generally is based on their new scholarly edition. However, in some of it unstylistic editorial slurs have crept in masked as originals – Brandenburg Concerto No. 1 springs to mind. Because performing editions generally are still untrustworthy, some people make their own material by copying from the Collected Editions of the full scores. However, except in rare cases, this is unnecessary, unless one wishes to preserve for one's own future use the results of the thought and labour which may have gone into editing orchestral parts for performance. To help those who do not wish to indulge in such laborious operations, there follows information (up-dated to 1979) about hiring and purchasing possibilities.

Belwin Mills sell large and small full scores of the following cantatas:

1, 4, 6, 11, 12, 17, 19, 21, 23, 27, 29, 30, 34, 46, 50, 51, 54, 56, 61, 62,65, 68, 78, 79, 80, 81, 82, 84, 93, 95, 102, 104, 105, 106, 113, 117, 120, 131, 137, 140, 144, 147, 149, 151, 155, 158, 159, 169, 172, 176, 178, 182, 186, 195, 201, 202, 205, 211 and 212.

They also sell orchestral parts for these works. At the present time they are considering putting this material into their hire library.

Novello do not sell any full scores or orchestral parts of Bach's works, but they do hire them for all the works that they publish (see Appendix B, List D). Futhermore, their hire library includes material from other publishers too.

Breitkopf and Härtel publish orchestral parts of all the cantatas; some can be bought, some are only on hire and at the time of writing their hire library is suffering some difficulties, but enquiries are invited. As already mentioned, Breitkopf's more recent publications are clear, clean and very readable. Naturally, coming from Germany, they are not cheap in the U.K.; at least three weeks should be allowed between ordering and delivery of orchestral material. This firm also issues a special cantata catalogue.

The full miniature scores published by Eulenberg are given in Appendix B, List F; no other performing material is available from this firm.

The cantatas available for purchase or hire in full and vocal scores and with orchestral parts from Hänssler of Stuttgart are given in Appendix B, List G.

The large public libraries which contain the complete full scores in the BG edition and the as yet incomplete NBA edition will usually lend them. For instance, the Central Music Library, housed by Westminster Library in Buckingham Palace Road, SW1, has two sets of the BG and one of the NBA. There is a system by which material from this very large music library can be loaned to other libraries.

Virtually all the performing material from the firms mentioned above include keyboard realisations, but these are (a) often inaccurate and (b) in the case of Breitkopf sometimes divided between an organ part which simply doubles the voices, and a *cembalo* part which is a realisation of the figured harmonies of the orchestral sections. Those embarking on the exciting exploration of the cantatas — or indeed of any other baroque works — for the first time may perhaps need reminding that this music is quite incomplete without the correct realisation of the figured or unfigured harmonies, and that the proper continuo instrument for church music is organ, and for secular music, harpsichord. Finally, there is, happily, an increasing number of students now who are studying continuo realisation and are keen to practise their skills.

3
INTERPRETATION

It would be presumptuous, very stupid, and impossible to attempt to deal with all aspects of interpretation in one chapter of a very short book. What follows is a potted guide to the technical problems and a few general thoughts on the musical ones, although in practice these are not separable. A comprehensive treatment of the former is to be found in Robert Donington's *A Performer's Guide to Baroque Music*[1].

(a) Early eighteenth century performance practice and the problems it poses today[2]

Performing early eighteenth century music in the late twentieth century creates problems. The reasons for this can be summarised as follows.

The texture of the music is linear, therefore it is essential that each strand of it should be clearly heard. Much of it is in dance form, so it must have a lilt, and heaviness in performance must be avoided; this isn't easy with modern instruments.

The scores and parts handed down to us do not represent in final detail all that the composers intended, because so many conventions, unkown to most of us, were well known to performers of the time; for example, the universal practice of ornamenting certain cadences, or 'altering' certain note values so as to agree rhythmically with patterns in other voices. It was unnecessary to waste time putting down on paper what everyone would know. This applies to almost every movement of Handel, and only slightly less universally to Bach. What was not 'put down on paper' is what we therefore have to try and find out.

If every problem had only one right solution, as some would have us believe, a great deal of the fascination and challenge of tackling a baroque piece would fly out of the window — as would a lot of the work involved also! Because, even at this distance of time since the publication of Arnold Dolmetsch's pioneering book, *The Interpretation of seventeenth and eighteenth century music*[3], many people are still unaware of the problems it discusses, or even that there are problems, I will list some of them below, prior to a detailed discussion of each of those mentioned:

1 Bowing and tonguing
2 Dynamics
3 *Tempi*
4 Pauses
5 Ornamentation
6 Rhythmic 'alteration'

1 *Bowing and tonguing*
Although separate bows and tonguing for wind for each note could be regarded as a kind of 'norm' because a great deal of music was played in that way and it makes for maximum clarity in contrapuntal textures, obviously many works of the period also come to life only when articulated with slurs and *staccatos* in a nice proportion. Bach usually, but not quite always, indicated such marks *somewhere* in a piece, but not necessarily at the first appearance of the phrase(s) in question, unfortunately! The thoughts I have about this and the procedure to adopt run roughly on these lines:
(i) Using an *urtext* score such as the *Neue Bach Ausgabe* or *Bachgesellschaft*, first look at the instrumental parts of the piece to be performed to see if the composer has indicated any slurs or *staccato* marks at all.
(ii) If there are any, notice whether they concern actual themes and if so whether they are marked consistently at every appearance of them; this is rather unlikely to be the case.
(iii) If the answer to point (i) is negative, then the vocal parts may suggest that slurs could be effectively added to the instrumental voices of similar themes in a manner which would reflect the word underlay. If there is much doubling of instruments and vocal lines it is often, though not always, wise to make the articulation agree; however, as stated above, even in fairly slow-moving music greater clarity will frequently be obtained if instruments articulate separate notes while voices have *melismas*, especially if the bass department is involved. In rapid runs at any pitch it is certainly true, though a workable compromise can be for the woodwind

to play *legato* while the strings in unison with them bow separately; an example where this procedure applies effectively is the *Cum sancto spiritu* from Bach's Mass in B minor, bars 21 and 22 (violin 1, flutes and oboes), see Fig. 2 which is also a good example of the inconsistency one often finds. Again, there may be no need to add slurs at all if the composer has not directly or indirectly suggested any: certainly the splashing of *legato* indications piecemeal and without reason all over scores of early music by romantically-minded editors of the past was one of the worst features of their work.

Fig. 2

Mass in B minor, Cum Sancto spiritu, bars 21-22

(iv) If the answer to point (i) is affirmative, one's task is to see that the composer's intentions are marked consistently, that is of course assuming that the composer has not already done so, see Fig. 3 where slurs suggested by analogy are in brackets.

Fig. 3

Oboe da Caccia   Cantata 27, III, bars 9 & 10

If, as sometimes happens, he appears to have marked similar passages inconsistently (I say 'appears to have marked' because he could have dictated marks at rehearsals to be inserted in the parts by the players which were incorrectly understood), one has to decide which version he meant, see Fig. 4.

Sometimes ideas closely derived from a theme to which

Fig. 4

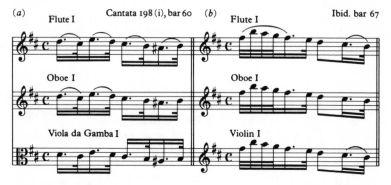

phrasing marks have been added, appear without any such marks; decisions have to be made on this point too, of which Bach's cantata BWV 92 (first movement) provides a good example; it is also a case where vocal *melismas* suggest instrumental slurring.

(v) The character of the music must always be a guide if one is taking the bold step of initiating phrasing marks for which there is no certain authority.

(vi) Sometimes one just *has* to hear a passage in rehearsal in particular conditions before being sure that a right decision has been made — and one may never be sure.

(vii) It is better to err on the side of too many separate notes than too many played *legato*.

(viii) All these points, and others, mainly concerning consistent ornamentation are admirably illustrated in Bach's Christmas Oratorio number 36 (first chorus of Part IV) NBA edition.

2 Dynamics

A convention that is not always understood is the following: at the instrumental beginning of a solo piece with orchestra there is usually an absence of any dynamic indication, but at the entry of the voice *p* or *piano* will certainly appear in some or all of the instrumental parts. If such a mark is omitted where it is needed it must certainly be put in; if it is simply delayed by a bar or two, look for a musical explanation. When the voice rests with the coming of the next instrumental *ritornello*, *f* or *forte* marks will appear as the *p* ones did, or should have done, when the voice part began; and so on throughout the movement. However, in practice, while preserving the basic contrasts, no performers are going to treat every movement as starting *f*, and from what one reads of baroque performances, it seems certain that musicians of those days would not have done so either. Probably the main purpose of these marks was to tell the players where the vocal entries were, so that they could listen and reduce the amount of tone suitably. Furthermore, if, for example, a cello and contrabass form the continuo part to an *obbligato* flute, it is reasonable to mark them down at least to *mf* if the flute is playing *f* and to keep that ratio to whatever may be the dynamic level of the flute; in such a case one might omit the contrabass since the choice of continuo instruments is always a flexible one. In other words, one must not be slavishly and unmusically literal in interpreting these dynamics. Like bowing and tonguing, many dynamics which the composer intended, but which are not fully marked in the scores, can be deduced by analogy, or from an indication in one or two voices, either vocal or instrumental – one group can take a cue from another as it undoubtedly did in earlier times.

Frequently one finds needed dynamic marks are absent; these have to be inserted: cantata 63 provides good examples. In the first duet, the solo oboe part has several marks, the continuo none; in bar 123 of the next (alto and tenor) duet violins and violas are marked *pp*, but the continuo has no indication although the last mark, bar 77, is *forte*.

Dynamics should only be *added* to clarify textures, underline climaxes, bring out echo effects which may seem to be inherent in the music and, naturally, to help phrasing, which I use here to mean maintaining momentum by working towards and away from strong beats. As regards tied notes involving suspensions, these must be held so that the 'crunch'

33

can be heard, as dissonance is a prime factor in propelling the music forward; I find that writing *ten* (short for *tenuto*) in the parts produces better results than the more common hairpins do.

The chief thing to bear in mind regarding dynamics is that any baroque movement has an essential unity stemming from the fact that it is monothematic; this statement must be amplified by pointing out that the one basic theme which gives the movement its single mood will probably have several counterthemes which combine with it (if it is composed by Bach), but which are similar in character; it may also have a contrasting theme in a different part of the movement; this often happens when Bach wants to highlight some passage which occurs later in the text – for example when the third and fourth lines of the text are contrasted with the first and second; often a movement may have two distinct sections (structurally, these often resemble a prelude and fugue, and a good example is the first movement of cantata BWV 46). Contrasted sections can have contrasted dynamics of course; the important point is that dynamics should underline and not obscure the structure or texture of the movement by violent contrasts which are alien to its nature. Recently I heard a performance of the *Agnus Dei* from the Mass in B minor sung expressively with *mf* – *mp* dynamics until the final instrumental *ritornello*, which was played with a fat and *forte* tone entirely at variance with anything which had gone before in the movement; this produced a jarring effect which spoilt the general mood of the piece.

Some people search around for places in a score where they can add to the composer's marks (written and implied), believing that the result will be dull if the score is left as it is. This is only partially true; the first essential is certainly to shape the phrases, and this may mean some additional marks; otherwise, most of the dynamic contrasts *are in the music*, and one only has slightly to underline and emphasise these and clarify the contrapuntal texture (and perhaps even these procedures may be unneccessary), to understand the mood of the movement as a whole, and otherwise to respect the composer's marks. Any other course will focus the attention on aspects foreign to the true nature of the work, like changes of mood and colour from phrase to phrase, something which does not exist in this music.

The sad fact is that countless amateur conductors, 'amateur' because their main musical calling is an academic or administrative one or even one which is entirely divorced from music, can be completely out of touch with modern thinking about performance practice, and in bouts of uncontrolled enthusiasm can litter their scores with romantic *crescendi* and *diminuendi*. These can be completely at variance with the structure of the music, and therefore fail to deliver its message in a manner which is intelligible to most musical people today. An instance of this was another performance of the Mass in B minor recently heard, but with different forces and a different conductor from that mentioned above, in which, for example, the *Et incarnatus*, one of the most mono-thematic pieces imaginable, ranged from *piano* to *forte* or *fortissimo* in every phrase, obliterating the orchestra and, instead of giving a feeling of profound awe at the mystery of the Incarnation, simply made this listener feel rather distressed.

3 Tempi

Most scholars agree that the relating of speeds which was the basis of tempi in earlier times had not been completely forgotten in the time of Bach. If one ignores the principle of relating the *tempo* of one section to another within a single movement or in a through-composed type of cantata the results are likely to sound jerky. Many conductors find that they naturally do relate *tempi* without consciously thinking about it. For illustration, take the *Sanctus* from the Mass in B minor: at the beginning of the fugue *pleni sunt coeli* the quaver triplets of the first section (*Sanctus*) could well become the normal quavers of the second section, that is, the new dotted crotchet will equal the previous crotchet. Similarly, at the end of the first section of the *Gloria* of the same work, by conducting a *hemiola* in the last two (³⁄₈) bars (i.e. three crotchets), one arrives at a suitable crotchet pulse for the next section (*Et in terra pax*), see Fig 5. The question of a single basic beat for a whole work is one that should not be dismissed as impractical musicological nonsense. Although

35

musical performances in general may not work by rules of this kind, many baroque pieces do, and the idea should be borne in mind when thinking about *tempi*, but it is certainly wrong to make a fetish of a consistent pulse if it does not suit the meaning of any particular movement as I have heard some young conductors do. Bach's motet *Jesu, meine Freude* and his cantata *Christ lag in Todesbanden* are convincing when performed with a consistent pulse throughout, perhaps because they are both really sets of variations.

Fig. 5   Mass in B minor Gloria, bars 99-101

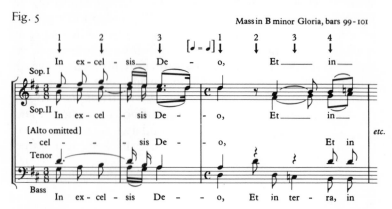

Many words used to indicate *tempi* today once had other meanings; in the baroque period often they were indications of mood rather than speed, the latter being suggested by the time signature and the note values. For example three semibreves in a bar ($\frac{3}{1}$) meant 'very quickly', and modern editions which translate this into $\frac{3}{2}$ or $\frac{3}{4}$ without saying what the original was are unhelpful. Above all, regard every metronomic or other indication of *tempo* in the standard performing vocal scores of Bach as highly suspicious or completely wrong. They are mostly the work of unenlightened nineteenth century editors.

Choice of *tempi* is very much a personal matter; there are surely no absolutes here. Apart from the well known fact that C. P. E. Bach said his father's tempi were on the fast side, the right *tempi* can depend on many factors. One should pause a long time before declaring another person's *tempi* too fast or too slow. A *tempo* is demonstrably too fast if singers or players cannot negotiate the notes clearly, the phrasing sounds rushed or breathless, the effect is blurred because of resonant acoustics, or the mood suggested by the words or title is destroyed – but of course there can be more than one valid intepretation of what the words suggest in Bach. A *tempo* is too slow if it is the cause of laboured phrasing, and again if it gives an effect contrary to the mood or style demanded by the words. But even here critics of other people's performances must be careful; a *tempo* may mean one thing to one person and something rather different to another. Some interpreters are too strongly influenced by recordings, which may be bad and unstylish. It has even been known for musicians to be influenced by editorial *tempo* indications in modern performing editions without realising that they *are editorial*. Many sensible remarks about *tempi* and interpretation generally can be found in *Musical Interpretation* by Sir Jack Westrup[4].

4 Pause marks in Bach's chorales

I have always believed that the meaning of these was obvious in the light of those in the *Orgelbüchlein* (where the chorale has pause marks but the surrounding counterpoint cannot stop); in other words, that they only mark the ends of phrases and did not imply any lengthening of time values. There seems to be little or nothing written in the seventeenth or eighteenth centuries on the subject, presumably because no one dreamed of doubting the meaning of the *fermata* sign in the context of chorales. But a little research which I did recently led me to some articles that confirm my opinion. F. Noske, in *Die Musikforschung* Vol. 17 (1964) pp. 383-8, briefly traces the history of the meaning of the *fermata* sign (and includes an instance from the *Orgelbüchlein* because there it *cannot* mean pause) and in summing up states (p.388) that there can be six different meanings, the fourth of which he gives as an 'ending (of phrase) sign (without any effect on the duration)'. J. Lee, in 'Interpreting the *Fermata*' in *The Instrument*, edited by John M. Christie, Evanston, Illinois, September 1969, discusses mainly the conductor's problems in more recent music, but adds, 'Many scholars consider the *fermata* in a Bach chorale not to be a long pause but only an indication of cadence points'. Dr. Bullivant also, in *Musical*

Times, December 1968, p.1149, asks, 'Why should conductors have to explain that these pause marks must be ignored?' *Das Alte Werk* (Telefunken records) has embarked on the first series of complete recordings of Bach cantatas using old instruments. They claim to be authentic in the proper sense and their performances are free in the treatment of chorale 'pauses'.

All this means that one should exercise common sense, pausing when the sense or exigencies of breathing demand it, and going on, even to joining phrases with a single breath, when the meaning of the text suggests it.

5 Ornamentation*

A list of all seventeenth and eighteenth century ornaments and the various ways of indicating them would fill many pages. The most useful books are Robert Donington's *The Interpretation of Early Music*[5] and *A Performer's Guide to Baroque Music*[1]; Walter Emery's excellent book *Bach's Ornaments*[6] is specifically for Bach. Here we are chiefly concerned with the trill, the *appoggiatura*, the slide and the mordent. The usual signs for these are as follows:

trill: *t*, *tr*, ∿, ∿∿ (plain); with specified prefixes and closing notes: ∿∿, ∿∿, ∿∿, ∿∿, ∿∿, ∿∿ .

Appoggiatura: a small note usually ♪ or ♪ above or below the principal note, or a single or double hook ∪ or ∪ above or below the principal note; the sign ♪ was never used. Slurs are usually added.

Slide: two small notes or ∿ placed below the principal note.

Mordent: ∿

Inexperienced performers of baroque music need to know (i) how to interpret ornaments indicated by the composer, and (ii) when to introduce additional ornaments.

(i) How to interpret ornaments indicated by the composer. The answer depends so much on context, *tempo*, instrument

*Since this chapter was written an important book has appeared which should be consulted if anyhow possible. This is *Ornamentation in Baroque and Post-Baroque Music with special emphasis on J. S. Bach* by Frederick Neumann, Princeton, University Press, 1979.

and countless unpredictable conditions, that giving a short final answer in any given situation would often be impossible, and explaining all the possibilities very space-consuming. The reader is referred to Walter Emery's *Bach's Ornaments*[6] for an eminently sensible approach. Emery quotes and gives examples – often contradictory – from various manuscripts, editions and authorities, discusses them and suggests possible solutions. Here one can give a few general directions and interpretations of certain common examples. In almost every case, the somewhat rare *Nachschlag* being an exception, Bach's ornaments start *on* the beat; slides and *appoggiaturas* should sound unhurried, the former, especially, are expressive embellishments and sound ludicrous if rushed, and can sound positively vulgar if played before the beat (see the opening phrase of *Erbarme dich*, No. 47 (39), from St Matthew Passion). This is not just a personal opinion, it is because popular music associations are called up if a slide is rushed and sounds like a scoop.

The length of an *appoggiatura* depends on the quality of the discord created, the surrounding harmony and the length of other *appoggiaturas* in the vicinity. In J. S Bach's music, so far as is known, the length of the (given) small note has nothing to do with the length of the *appoggiatura*[7]; although discussing possibilities in different situations can seem complicated, solutions are usually simple and obvious. There are no blanket rules, but the following may be helpful:

An *appoggiatura* seldom takes more than half the value of the main note except in compound time, where it can often take two-thirds or the whole value, with the resolution coming on the next beat if it is a rest. Another exception could be those in the opening bars of the duet, No. 33 in the St Matthew Passion, where I find that crotchets are more in keeping than quavers or semi-quavers with what I believe to be the mood of the piece, namely a nasty, quick-moving ugly scene. For harmonic and other reasons it may take far less than half, but will never approximate to a 'crushing note'. *Appoggiaturas* before trills occurring on dotted quavers, crotchets or minims nearly always take one-third of the value of the principal note (see below re trills).

A trill can have 'opening notes' and/or 'closing notes', or neither; its length obviously depends on the length of the principal note and on the *tempo*; the signs for a trill given above do not relate very much to its length or to whether it has a prefix or a suffix as, to quote Emery again, 'when Bach used the wavy line sign he did not count the humps in it'[8], and 'eighteenth century copyists seem sometimes to have replaced Bach's complex shake signs (ᴧᴧᴧ, ᴜᴧᴧᴧ etc., specifying appoggiaturas and prefixes) by the "plain" tr'[9]. It can depend on the time allowed and the mood as to which interpretation one adopts. Practical solutions, especially in choral trills, are to have a short *appoggiatura* and short trill finishing on a beat or half-beat, with perhaps a short anticipatory note before the next principal one, but in such a case one should look at what the other instruments and/or voices may be doing at the same moment: it makes sense to see that everyone does the same. It should be remembered that all but the shortest and fastest single shake – trills ('schneller') should start on the upper note.* One example of the commonest trill situation must suffice:

Fig. 6

and similarly with dotted crotchet and quaver or a dotted minim and crotchet.

The mordent is simply a single inverted trill, namely with only one repercussion, in fact the equivalent of what is today called an inverted mordent.

Bach's own and only 'Explication' should be consulted; it is easily available in his *Clavierbüchlein* for his eldest son Wilhelm Friedmann Bach. A good guide to it is given in Emery's book pp. 13-15 (see note 6 above).

Finally, although in any one movement or section of a movement it is a laudable ideal to aim at achieving uniformity in the interpretation of ornaments, making a

*But the conclusions of the author of the most recent book on this subject, by Frederick Neumann (see page 38), are that many of Bach's trills should start on the principal note.

fetish of it can be counter-productive in that it can destroy the feeling of spontaneity which is of the essence of all embellishments. Even a brief study of some of Bach's keyboard works provides convincing proof that Bach himself could not have always been consistent in performances; e.g. some trills indicated in the opening statement of a fugue subject which can or should be played as full-length trills simply cannot be so rendered at every subsequent entry in the movement.

(ii) When to introduce additional ornaments.
The introduction of additional ornaments is less necessary in Bach than in many other baroque composers because he incorporated so much embellishment into his music; his great critic, Adolf Scheibe, in fact complained bitterly about this. Nevertheless, like all composers of his time, Bach usually worked in a hurry, and so did not always write in what would have been obvious to performers familiar with the conventions of the time. For instance, trills at all the main cadences (especially those involving ♩♫ or ♩. ♪) are frequently left out or only occasionally indicated, but they should be regarded as obligatory[10]; see Fig. 7a, b, c, d, e and f. In Fig. 7f the trumpet is playing the main (fugue) subject of the movement and the presence of the trill in bar 43 confirms the view that the subject should be similarly embellished from the (vocal) beginning of the fugal section. Musically, cadential trills are important in adding extra dissonance and maintaining melodic animation at the ends of phrases. In any case, as with bowing and tonguing marks, it is largely a matter of getting consistency by analogy. If an ornament is an integral part of a musical theme there is a case for it to be added on all occasions (but see above, namely the final paragraph of section (i)).

The lesson to be learned from Fig. 8a and b is less obvious. In the light of the last sentence of the previous paragraph, one might add a slide before the A flat in bar 2 (Fig. 8a) by analogy with bar 62 (Fig. 8b), but another viewpoint could be that the theme should grow in intensity through additional embellishments as the movement progresses, in which case one could take a hint from the

Fig. 7

Fig. 8

vocal lines and add an appoggiatura to the fifth note of the
theme in later occurrences as well as a slide to the ninth note of
it. The sixth movement of cantata 134 (NBA edition)
provides interesting cases where ornaments are called for by
analogy *and for the right musical effect* (see bars 172–4, 228–230,
and 274–5). The same movement provides food for thought
on a subject much discussed in recent years in America,
namely, the use of solo singers within a chorus movement. All
that space in this book allows for is the generalisation that this
practice is rare in Bach, occurring only in cantatas 21, 24, 71,
76, 110, 134 and 195 according to the late Walter Emery, and
that Bach usually left directions about *Concertante* effects if he
wanted them, as he did in cantata 21. In this movement from
cantata 134, where the two-part passages are marked *senza
violone* in the continuo, and *p* or *pp* in another instrumental part
(here additional marks are called for by analogy), Bach
probably intended solo voices; an additional reason for this
supposition is that the cantata was originally for a wedding

(134a) when Bach might have had more singers available, and these marks may be a hang-over from that version.

6 Rhythmic 'alteration'

'Interpretation of modern rhythmic signs in the light of seventeenth and eighteenth century writings and conventions' might be a more accurate heading for this section. The double dot had not been invented when Bach and his contemporaries were composing; and the ♩ ₃ ♪ sign is very rare. In addition, the essence of rhythm in the period was its flexibility[11], whereas in today's music, the exact opposite holds good. Ever since the publication of Prout's edition of *Messiah* about a century ago few people have questioned the alteration of ♩ ♪ ♫ to ♩. ♪ ♫ in 'Surely Thou hast borne our griefs.' It took until about the middle of the twentieth century and Dolmetsch's *The Interpretation of seventeenth and eighteenth century music* in the second decade[3] and Dart's *The Interpretation of Music* in the fifth decade[12], however, for any serious move to be made towards applying the principles governing such alteration to baroque music generally. These principles are more concerned with the alignment of rhythms in any one movement or section than with double-dotting. Several scholars have recently questioned double dotting first movements of French Overtures and certainly if these are taken at a brisk *tempo* it can be unnecessary. This does not mean that alignment of rhythms should be ignored; double or even triple dotting of crotchets in a prevailing dotted quaver-semi-quaver situation might be called for in order to obtain the necessary crisp and tidy effect.

In a movement where triplets are dominant all other rhythms tend to agree, even ♫ could become ♩ ₃ ♪. The *Sanctus* from the Mass in B minor and verse VI of cantata 4 (*Christ lag in Todesbanden*) are well known pieces that give food for thought on this subject. In the former, if the *tempo* is very slow, the printed rhythms could work, and a majestic effect – given the right building – could result, though my view is that alignment, that is, ♩♩♩ (trumpets) plus ♩ ₃ ♪ (violins and violas) plus ♩ ♫ (timpani), is more

43

satisfactory at any speed. In cantata 4, verse VI, many years
of performances, experimentation, and listening to other
people's versions have convinced me that the whole
movement as $\frac{12}{8}$ (♩. ♪ and ♫ as ♩ 𝟛 ♪) at a brisk *tempo*
— about ♩(·) = 96 — is the only way fully to convey the joyous
mood implied by the words.

As stated near the beginning of this chapter there are few
finally 'correct' solutions to these problems, and one always
needs to keep a thoughtful, open mind. Before closing this
section I would mention one particularly intractable
problem, namely the tenor aria in cantata 119. Two
professional performances and many seminars on it seem to
show that the totally $\frac{12}{8}$ solution is the right one because the
reference in the text to the Linden trees (of Leipzig) suggests
that they might be swaying in the wind and triplets certainly
portray this. But another viewpoint, put to me by an
eminent American musicologist who, however, had not
performed the work, was that one should over-dot the ♩. ♪ of

Fig. 9

Mass in A, IV bars 106-8

the first section and under-dot the same rhythm (making triplets) when the written triplets appear later.

Fig. 9 gives the strongest proof of the need to alter some of the printed rhythms in the cause of musical sense, in this case uniformity in the pattern of the four vocal entries. Only in the alto part could Bach write the precise rhythm he intended without double dotting; yet these other voices and the orchestral context leave no doubt as to what he meant.

Further illustrations of most of the above points are given in articles by the present writer in *The Musical Times*, May, June, and July 1958.

(b) From the purely musical viewpoint

This is not so much a separate consideration of interpretation but a setting out of reasons for taking this or that decision in the matters discussed in section (a).

It may appear insulting to the reader to make such an obvious ruling that *tempi*, dynamics and phrasing must spring from the performer's reaction to the words (*and* to the music, although this will normally agree with the reaction to the words); there are of course several ways of interpreting some of Bach's religious texts. Many cantata words express ideas with which it is not always easy to identify oneself today, yet running through these words, and far more so through the music which generally transcends the text, one usually finds a message with which one *can* identify; in any case, it is part of an artist's job to do so, however difficult the task. It is of course far easier to get personally involved in the major works like the Passions, Masses and Christmas Oratorio, where the Bible and Liturgy play a larger part. Yet in this secular age one hears many performances of these works where the *tempi* and general style seem to have no bearing on what the words are trying to tell one, but seem more connected with some bogey like maintaining a consistent pulse for a whole section of a whole cantata, whether it really 'works' for each movement or not. This is the only explanation I can offer for rushed *Kyrie eleisons* (for example No. 1 in the Mass in B minor), unrestful, hurried lullabies (for example No. 19 in the Christmas Oratorio), and jolly, 'weeping' arias (from the Passions) that are constantly heard today. All this may sound smug and out-of-date, but it should be remembered that most of the works we are dealing with were composed for a church service, and the majority of them to illuminate the gospel for the day; they were a commentary on it of equal importance with the sermon. In fact I would argue that Bach is the greatest preacher of all time! Naturally, deciding what his message is must be a subjective matter, and all that is being suggested here is that the text as well as the musical language in which it is clothed (and misfits are very rare) be given the highest priority when studying a score and preparing for its interpretation. This is what seems to be lacking in some 'authentic' performances and recordings, which is particularly sad, as they should be able to get most easily to the heart of the music. The late Sir Henry Wood, whose Bach performances were inflated and romantic by today's standards, but who littered his scores with very perceptive remarks, once said 'When I am going to conduct the St Matthew Passion I first study the story in the gospel'.

Although it may appear to conflict with the points just made, one must also bear in mind that most baroque movements contain a strong dance element: many of them are in definite dance form and some are so labelled, even when they are wedded to 'sacred' words. This is why a lightweight style of interpretation is so essential. Every individual may feel any given piece in a different way; but the essential thing is that one must feel it in *some* way through study, there being no short cuts to good phrasing or any of the finer points of interpretation. However, the following may be helpful.

Since most singers and players, whether professional or amateur, solo or with a group, tend to stress equally every beat of every bar in Bach's music, one has to encourage them to grade the pulses tonally towards the strong points. This bad habit does not necessarily mean that they are unmusical; it is because there has been, and, sadly, still is in Germany, a long tradition of regarding the music's so called 'sewing machine rhythms' as needing pounding stresses on every one of those endless bars of quaver continuo parts with which the music abounds. The real rhythmic life in Bach's music, and it has more than its fair share compared with that of other men, lies in the *harmonic* rhythm,* and this again moves to and from the many crunching discords on the natural strong beats which propel the music forward. This, incidentally, is why all such discords, if they are suspended, must be held (no breaths, no stopping or lifting of the bow) if the music is to make sense (see earlier in this chapter in Section (a) 2, where the same point is approached from a different angle).

Put in simple practical terms, this means: reduce the number of accents to one in every bar or, better still, every two, three, or four bars, and always work towards and away from those accents.

*As well as in the more obvious melodic rhythm of course.

4
SOLOISTS

To keep the order of chapters in this book as far as possible identical with the order of events in planning and organising a concert, choosing vocal soloists must now be considered. For Bach the choices are not very wide, for singers with huge uncontrolled *vibratos* are not suitable because they cannot create clear lines, and so textures sound muddled. In fact, a quartet of singers all with *vibratos* of different speeds and widths can make the simplest harmonies sound unrecognisable! With this type of singer intonation is often suspect too. Bach taxes any performer's musicianship to such an extent that a singer whose reading and general musicality is insecure will give the conductor constant cause for anxiety. Fortunately, today in Britain we have a lot of very reliable singers (many tenors and basses are ex-choral scholars from Oxbridge), and with their excellent musical equipment goes, in most cases, a healthy attitude to performance. In other words, they are more interested in singing good music well than in earning the highest possible fees. However, a singing life is not very long; therefore soloists' fees have to rise faster than the cost of living. Having said which, a word of warning must be given. At the time of writing singers' agents tend, quite naturally, to raise the fees of those they represent at an alarming rate, far outstripping the rate of increases in funds from grant-giving bodies, and this, time and time again, without the knowledge of the singers concerned. I am not criticising every manifestation of this policy, for I fully understand the reasons for it, but I am implying that it can be counter-productive.

Front-rank soloists need to be booked eighteen months to two years before the concert; other good ones *at least* a year in advance. At the time of booking it is advisable to give as much detail as possible about rehearsal(s). Almost every good singer is only too pleased to give a preliminary piano rehearsal a week or two before the concert in order to settle such essential matters as *tempi*, ornamentation and general style; otherwise, time will be wasted at the final rehearsal and, far worse, disagreements and frustrations may occur which cannot but be detrimental to performance. If distances are too great or work pressures too exhausting for personal meetings, a great deal can be done by letter or telephone or both.

5
ORCHESTRA

Some aspects of using an orchestra were covered in earlier chapters. Here we shall be concerned with balance, style and choice of instruments.

(a) Balance with choir and soloists

A large amateur choir of voices with weak and unfocussed tone does not make such a powerful sound as a good well-trained (amateur) group of possibly one third of the size; therefore the numbers of string players (wind will very seldom be doubled) cannot be in any fixed ratio to the number of singers. For a reasonably good choir of fifty to seventy voices a string strength of five first violins, four seconds, three violas, two cellos, and one bass is sufficient; having two basses depends on the work, the acoustics, whether a bassoon is present and also on whether the bass player is playing a modern or an old bass or a *violone* (which blends well with modern strings); if a *violone*, then two will be needed. With an orchestra larger than this one can consider reducing the number of desks in some of the solo items. If all instruments are baroque, more will be required to balance. Which brings us to the whole question of authenticity.

(b) Modern or baroque instruments?

The point is still raised that we should use modern instruments and styles for old music because Bach and others would have appreciated them if they had had them, and would have written for them. Possibly they would, although as the late Sir Jack Westrup states[1] 'Bach did not like the pianos he came across'. What knocks the bottom out of the argument is the certainty that if the great composers of the past had had our instruments they would have written different sorts of music. Most of them were, after all, highly professional people, and understood precisely the sounds and capabilities of the instruments and voices for which they wrote. Any other viewpoint presupposes the belief that all art progresses – a doubtful and embarrassing theory if pushed too far.

Achieving clarity with modern instruments and large choirs is extremely difficult. The larger the choir, the less homogeneity of tone and the more doubtful intonation will result, and those two factors produce muddy textures. Nearly all twentieth-century orchestral instruments are high-powered versions of their forebears, prepared so as to produce a large sound and a strong, hard attack when needed; strings and woodwind are played normally with much *vibrato* at all times, which is probably the greatest destroyer of clear textures in baroque music; and this *molto vibrato* unconsciously becomes a substitute for careful intonation and phrasing, especially the latter, for if every note makes a high emotional impact, it is hard for it to form a part of a phrase in this kind of music. One has only to listen to some of the German recordings of early works (especially works by Schütz) to see how *not* to achieve good phrasing and a springy dance rhythm. Much can be done with small choral forces and intelligent use of modern instruments. I suppose small choirs have been recognised for at least a generation or two now as ideal for early music, but the message about style and playing has only comparatively recently got across to instrumentalists. I have however, been delighted to find that many groups of string players to whom I have suggested 'less vibrato and less attack' have all responded enthusiastically. Of course the use of old instruments is better still, though the British speaking countries have been slow to adopt them, and rightly, because the time taken to acquire a good technique is longer than most players in Britain can afford to give. At the time of writing therefore, there are only a few string players and even fewer wind players who are good musicians *and* excellent technicians on the early instruments or modern reproductions of them. When enough experts are at hand however, the result can be amazing, so many difficulties of phrasing vanishing immediately, for the great advantage of older bows is the ease of articulation and the dance-lilt which results. Sackbuts, clarino trumpets and *violones* will go with modern instruments in other sections; otherwise it is impossible to mix old and new.

Light flute stops and low pressure wind from the organ is another essential. I would go so far as to say that the open diapason stop family of a romantic organ, when used for continuo, does as much harm as anything to a clear true Bach texture. I am talking about organs and not harpsichords because the latter hardly figured in Bach's church music performances in normal conditions; arguments put forward in, for example, quite recent record sleeves do not hold water.

From what has been said, it will be clear that baroque instruments potentially give far the best and quickest musical results; but although phrasing is much easier, problems of intonation are great. Also, as the baroque oboe is built approximately a semitone lower than modern pitch, keyboard continuo instruments (and of course all others) have to come into line (chamber electronic organs are usually adjustable) and solo singers must be warned — they may have 'perfect pitch'. In the long term then, it depends on whether enough of the best baroque players in all sections are available on the date(s) in question and whether one can afford at least one extra instrumental rehearsal (because of intonation difficulties), as to whether it is worth risking 'going baroque'.

If, however, all authentic instruments are to be used, then it is essential that soloists — preferably all male — are chosen having straight clean tone to match, and that the choir — also preferably all male – is small; the maximum number being about thirty. Their tone should also be free from *vibrato*. This is too often forgotten in 'authentic' performances.

(c) **Unusual instruments and possible substitutes**

Some of these questions, for example *oboes da caccia*, and *viole d'amore* have already been covered (see Chapter 1).

Bach had a very fine ear for orchestral colour and created many ravishingly beautiful and original sounds; this side of his genius has not been sufficiently stressed, as anyone will testify who has heard such movements as the second tenor aria in cantata 107,* the tenor aria in cantata 95 or the opening chorale fantasia of cantata 8, to name the first three examples that spring to mind. Yet it always amazes me how well his music can sound using some of the wrong instruments. In most cases it is far better to substitute than not to perform the work at all. Slightly changing orchestral colours by substituting for one or two instruments is not nearly so drastic as ignoring a composer's intentions altogether, which happens in the innumerable performances with organ only of works composed with orchestral accompaniments. Yet it is arguable that even this is better than no performance — depending on how much of the original orchestral colour can be reproduced on the organ.

If recorders — indicated in the score by flauto = *blockflöte*, *flute dolce* — are not available, use transverse flutes – *querflöte* –; vice versa also works, but less successfully.

The *taille* which sometimes appears in the cantatas is a tenor oboe and is normally played today by a cor anglais.

If oboists have not access to *oboes d'amore*, and few players *own* them, oboes or cor anglais are the best substitutes, providing the range presents no problem. Bärenreiter orchestral parts usually have printed alternative versions for both these instruments. Many movements in the keys of A or D for *oboe d'amore* contain unplayable low A's which are important, being either tonic or dominant. Transposing the note or a whole phrase an octave higher can spoil the effect. Here musical ingenuity has to be brought to bear: Leave out the note? Spoil the contours and transpose part of the phrase? Spoil the colour and transpose the whole phrase? Use a cor anglais (will the *whole* part fit?)? Or cast purism to the winds and use a clarinet?

Two big problems are the *violino piccolo*, a small violin tuned a minor third higher (cantatas 96, 102 (optional), 140 and Brandenburg Concerto No.1) and the *violoncello piccolo*, a smaller cello tuned a fifth higher (cantatas 6, 41, 49, 68, 85, 115, 175, 180, and 183). There are very few of these instruments and players of them about. In some works their special colour seems more important than in others. For example, in cantata 6 the *cello piccolo* creates an exquisite

*Especially if on baroque instruments

sound with the soprano(s) and continuo. Moreover, the range of its *obbligato* renders it unsatisfactory on the ordinary cello and unplayable on the viola; on the other hand, in cantatas 68, 85, 115, and 175 the ordinary cello can work quite well. If, however, it does not seem comfortable, try a viola, or persuade the cellist to tune a three-quarter size cello up a fifth, and practise it. Except possibly in cantatas 6 and 183, there is no need to avoid performing the works because of the *violoncello piccolo* problem. Regarding obbligati for the *violino piccolo*, in cantata 96 Bach doubles it with a high recorder, so omission of the former is possible, though not desirable, and in cantata 102 he indicates a transverse flute as an alternative; this leaves the famous cantata 140, *Wachet auf.* Although true purists will be shocked, quite frankly, the big *obbligato*, number 3, can sound very well on a normal violin especially if it is a baroque one. Where I miss the small one — in every performance I can recall — is in the final chorale, where its thin, silvery tone playing the chorale an octave higher is delightful; a full size violin is too heavy.

Bach indicates *violone*, almost certainly at sixteen-foot pitch, against his continuo lines; this is the double bass of the viol family. As stated above, it blends well with the violin group but is weaker than the modern double bass. It does not have the tendency to aggressive attack, the death of good phrasing in baroque music, which bedevils so often the use of a modern bass. Playing with nearly every note *forte piano* is expected or asked for by many conductors of later music; the players are not to blame for using it on all occasions, but they need to be corrected.

A *viola da gamba* is scored for in cantatas 76, 106 (two), 152, 198 (two) and 205, lutes only in cantata 198 and St John Passion (one), see p. 5. In number 76 a *gamba* is an important *obbligato* instrument; in cantata 198 two lutes simply (but effectively) strengthen the keyboard continuo, but the two *gambas* are essential, as they are in cantata 106. There is no great shortage of players of these instruments, but a *gamba* can usually be substituted by a cello.* Bach's scoring in cantatas 16, 157, and 215 for a *violetta* can be ignored; this was an instrument similar to the viola and

___

*But the effect is totally different (see above re Passions).

apparently of the same compass. It appears either in unison with other strings (215), or as a viola substitute (157), or as an alternative to an *oboe da caccia* (16).

6
REHEARSING THE CHOIR

(a) General style

As will have been gathered from what has already been discussed, the important points to aim at in the choral singing of Bach are clarity and lively rhythms, for Bach's textures are often thick and a great deal of his music is dance-like. Broadly speaking, success is achieved through careful phrasing, dynamic balancing and by cultivating clean well-focussed tone, *senza vibrato*, from all performers.

(b) Chorales

Although these *may* have been sung congregationally — but the embellishments of many of the melodies suggest that they were not — there is every reason for treating them with sensitive verbal phrasing, avoiding four equally stressed beats in each bar, and with dynamic shading which will underline the meaning of the words, while avoiding anything that remotely resembles a Victorian part-song. If the top line is doubled by, say, two or more oboes and flutes and first violins, one or two of the wind could drop out in chorales or sections of chorales which are taken *piano*, in order to balance the choral singing; similarly with bassoon(s) or second desk cellos and basses, and so on. The scoring of the chorales does not strike one as being wholly sacrosanct in regard to doubling. As stated in Chapter 3(a), one does not have to stop rhythmically at pause marks; overall rhythmic shape, the need for breath and the sense of the words are the governing factors in deciding what to do.

(c) Fugues

Bach's works abound in fugues and fugal textures. Often the composer provides built-in contrasts and natural approaches to climaxes in tone through starting a vocal movement in fugal style without orchestral doubling, sometimes even with solo voices alone. If no such natural contrasts are provided, usually something can be worked out so that a movement builds up tonally to its natural structural climax *without starting it with a basically different dynamic* (and therefore mood) from that in which it will finish. A good general rule is to see that each fugue subject is followed by a slightly quieter dynamic when the next voice enters. Quick notes sung *semi-staccato* – but not completely *staccato* – greatly aid clarity and can sound brilliant; instrumentalists should produce this effect naturally, vocalists have to be told.

7
REHEARSING THE ORCHESTRA

It goes without saying that the first requisites for a successful rehearsal and concert are a thorough technical competence and knowledge of the score on the part of the conductor. It is therefore necessary for a conductor to practise his art, as players and singers must theirs. His primary task is to set and maintain correct *tempi* and enable people to start and finish together, and so on. Helpful books are numerous, but the greatest help can come from consulting a reliable and experienced orchestral musician of integrity, for example, the leader of a section, about such fundamental matters as where to put the tip of the stick (or fingers, if no stick is used), and what sort of beat various kinds of music demand. But this can require more courage and humility than most of us can muster. It depends on whether interpreting the music or self-importance comes first.

Too often, however, the mechanics of preparation are allowed to take priority over studying the music. Marking scores and orchestral material should be done weeks or months in advance, in fact such work can make a quite relaxing holiday task! Marking vocal scores should as far as possible be done at rehearsals, or delegated; marking orchestral material has to be so precise − or it is useless and only holds up a rehearsal − that it is unwise to delegate it to anyone other than a professional. Whenever a building other than a purpose-built concert hall is used for fairly large-scale music making, a great many changes have to be made to accommodate choir, orchestra and soloists so that all can see and be heard. Conductors must decide what the changes shall be, but should absolutely refuse to do any of the work themselves. Their job is to think in a relaxed manner about the music and how it will be rehearsed.

All rehearsals should be carefully planned; in Bach this is specially necessary because he, of all late baroque composers, probably used the greatest variety of instruments. Because he rang the changes on them so imaginatively, few movements have *tutti* scoring; many use only a very few players and one solo singer. Thus it is important both to save expense as well as to avoid boredom, frustration and waste of time, to plan rehearsals so that there is a minimum amount of sitting around for players who are *tacet*. In this way one can often rehearse quite a lot of music for little cost by paying overtime to two or three players (actually, the continuo group and one or two others). But one hour is the maximum allowed and it has to join on to a main rehearsal; it is important to see that the total rehearsal time is not such as will put too much strain on any of the performers; thus the maximum use can be made of the full main rehearsal(s). Working out a rehearsal schedule is a tiresome business, but it is well worth the effort; it should be done, of course, at the time of booking the orchestra.

At the beginning of this chapter the paramount importance of learning the scores was emphasised; one should in fact always try to achieve the ideal of memorising them. Of almost equal importance with this is the power to communicate with players and singers directly and quickly without loss of time or temper. Some people confuse rudeness with greatness; this can be a mistake of fatal proportions.

The following remarks apply to the one or perhaps two rehearsals that are all a choral conductor usually gets with an orchestra before a choral concert. They should not be mistaken for potted instructions on how to train an orchestra over a longer period.

Professional orchestral players are highly skilled musicians and deserve respect; they will give of their best when such respect, plus firmness and good manners are conveyed from the rostrum. *Never* talk to a professional orchestra about the music they are about to play *before* they play it. All they are interested in at the first run-through is playing the right notes in the manner required by the conductor, and that really sums it up. Therefore listen *first of all* for wrong notes and other technical errors, and also to balance, and *later* talk about musical matters. Intelligently marked parts and a good stick technique plus a verbal hint or two if necessary will get a lot of musical points right at the second run-through, which, if the notes were correct or corrected the first time, need not be a complete one, if time presses. In short, the best way to get respect and good results is to know the scores, be well organised, relaxed and polite. Tantrums get nowhere; they cause embarrassment and are usually a cover-up for incompetence.

The technique of dealing with an amateur orchestra is only slightly different: amateurs should be *expected* to get things right and indeed be treated like professionals as far as possible. The difference is that they may need teaching in some areas and require time to practise difficult passages slowly (professionals also sometimes need and ask for this).

Rapport with any group of singers or players depends always on the personality of the director. Difficult personalities cannot be fundamentally changed overnight, but they can improve by the practice of self-control.

APPENDIX A

Notes to Chapter 1

1 Edited by D. Hellmann, Stuttgart, 1964
2 A. Mendel: *Bach, Johannes-Passion*, Kassel 1973
3 W. Schmieder: *Bach-Werke Verzeichnis*, Leipzig 1958
4 A *gamba* in nos. 40 and 41 (34 and 35) and a harpsichord were only used with orchestra II in a performance late in Bach's time when the second organ was out of service.
5 The palindrome structure is explained in P. Steinitz: *Bach's Passions*, London, 1979 and in K. Geiringer: *J. S. Bach, The culmination of an era*, London 1967.
6 BWV 249a, *Entfliehet, verschwindet, entweichet, ihr Sorgen*.
7 In BG vol. 41 p. 187
8 Edited P. Steinitz, London 1970
9 See note 3 *supra*
10 The case against wholesale doubling of the motets with instruments has been well argued by Dr. Bullivant in *Bach Jahrbuch*, 1966, p. 59 (in German only).
11 See P. Steinitz: *Bach for Choirs*, London 1978

Notes to Chapter 2

1 Edited by P. Steinitz
2 London, 1959

Notes to Chapter 3

1 London, 1973
2 I am grateful to the Arts Council of Great Britain for their permission to use material in this chapter from an article I wrote in the *National Federation of Music Societies' Newsletter* in 1972; I also wish to thank the Editor of the *Choral Journal of America* for permission to use passages from an article I wrote for that magazine a few years ago.
3 London, 1915
4 BBC, London, 1971
5 London, 1963 and 1974
6 London, 1953
7 Ibid, p. 77
8 Ibid., p. 36
9 Ibid., p. 38
10 cf. Donington: The Interpretation of Early Music, op. cit. p. 178

11 See Donington: A Performer's Guide to Baroque Music, op. cit. p. 254
12 London, 1954

Notes to Chapter 5

1 Musical Interpretation, London, 1971, p. 62

APPENDIX B

List A gives a list of cantatas containing solo movement(s) which can effectively be sung chorally, or semi-chorally. The numbers in brackets indicate the movement(s) in question. A dagger after a number indicates that only a few voices should be used because of balancing with only a few instruments.

List A

Cantata number 2 (v), 4 (whole work), 6 (iii), 7 (ii and vi), 8 (iv), 10 (ii, iv and v), 12 (v), 13 (iii), 14 (iv)†, 17 (iii and v), 22 (ii)†, 25 (v), 27 (iii† and v), 28 (i), 29 (iii† and vii†), 34 (iii), 36 (ii†, iii, v and vi), 37 (iii), 38 (v), 39 (iv and v†), 41 (ii†) 44 (iii† and iv), 45 (iii, iv and v), 48 (iv† and vi), 61 (iii), 63 (v), 64 (v), 66 (iii and v†), 68 (ii†), 69 (iii†), 71 (ii and iv), 72 (iv), 74 (iv), 75 (iii), 78 (ii†), 79 (ii† and v), 80 (ii – soprano part – and iv†), 91 (v), 92 (iv and viii), 93 (iii, iv and vi), 95 (ii – chorale section†), 99 (v), 102 (iv), 104 (v), 106 (whole work), 111 (ii), 113 (ii and iii[16]), 115 (ii), 116 (iv) (but it is extremely difficult), 119 (v†), 120 (iv†), 120a (iii and vi), 123 (v), 124 (v), 125 (iv), 128 (iii – a good amateur soloist could manage the central recitative section of this fine aria – and iv), 129 (iii and iv), 130 (v†), 131 (whole work), 133 (ii and iv), 134 (iv), 135 (v), 136 (iii and v), 137 (ii and iii), 138 (v), 140 (iv), 141 (ii and iv), 143 (ii and vi), 145 (iii and v)[17], 146 (iii, v and vii), 147 (iii and ix), 148 (iv), 149 (iv and vi), 150 (whole work), 161 (iii), 172 (iii and iv), 173 (iii and iv), 176 (iii and v), 177 (iv or possibly the whole work), 178 (ii and iv), 179 (v), 180 (v), 181 (iii), 182 (iv), 184 (ii), 186 (viii and x), 187 (iii and iv), 194[18] (x), 196 (iv), 197 (iii).

List B★

Cantatas with more than one major choral movement. Cantata number 4★, 6★, 11★, 16, 21★, 23★, 34★, 39, 44, 46★, 48 (has a long chorus and two chorales, and except for two recitatives the whole work could be sung chorally), 50★ (single double choir movement), 61★, 63★, 64 (has one chorus and three chorales), 67, 68, 71, 79★ (barring one recitative, the whole work could be sung chorally), 80★, 92 (one chorus, two chorales, two arias singable chorally, leaving only tenor and bass needed as soloists), 95★, 106★, 118★ (single choral movement), 119, 131†, 138, 143, 150, 178, 182, 191★, 195★, 196 and 198† (a funeral ode, but strictly speaking, not a church cantata).

List C★

Solo Cantatas, including those with a finale chorale. Cantata number 13★, 32★, 35, 42, 49, 51★, 52★, 54, 55, 56, 57★, 58, 59, 60★, 81★, 82★, 83, 84★, 85★,

★Outstanding works are marked with a ★.

86, 87, 88*, 89, 90*, 132, 144, 151, 152, 153* (includes three splendid chorales), 154-8, 159*, 162-8, 169*, 170*, 174, 175*, 183, 184, 199*.

List D

Cantatas published by Novello. Cantata number 4, 6, 8, 11 (this is the Ascension Oratorio), 12, 21, 25, 27, 28, 34, 38, 39, 41, 43, 50, 61, 63, 67, 68, 70, 79, 80, 81, 93, 95, 104, 106, 112, 115, 116, 119, 140, 149, 180, 198 and 201.

List E

Cantata vocal scores *not published* by Belwin Mills (checked to 1979). Cantata number 2, 3, 10, 18, 23, 29, 30, 32, 37, 39, 40, 44, 46, 50, 51, 53 (not by Bach), 57, 63, 72, 73, 76, 78, 93, 117, 124, 126, 127, 128, 129, 130, 131, 133, 137, 152, 155, 159, 160 (not by Bach), 161, 167, 170, 171, 199, 200, 214, 215, 216, 217, 218, 219, 220, 221, 222 and 223.

List F

Cantata miniature scores, German texts, but some also with singable English published by Eulenberg (obtainable from Schott). Cantata number 1, 4, 6, 7, 8, 11, 12, 17, 19, 21, 23, 27, 28, 29, 31, 32, 34, 37, 38, 39, 40, 46, 50, 51, 54, 55, 56, 60, 61, 62, 66, 67, 68, 79, 80, 81, 85, 92, 93, 104, 105, 106, 117, 119, 123, 127, 131, 137, 140, 155, 158, 159, 161, 170, 179, 182, 205, 211 and 212.

List G

Cantatas published by *Hänssler of Stuttgart*, thirty-two in German, fourteen of which have alternative English. These are as follows, German only: cantata number 6, 11, 34, 50, 51, 65, 79, 80, 93, 104, 105, 106, 140, 151, 155, 161, 176, and 186; German and English: 17, 23, 27, 29, 32, 37, 61, 62, 78, 127, 131, 137, 158 and 159.

[16] Note that in cantata 113 (iii) there is a misprint in the Breitkopf vocal score in bar 23: the second note in the vocal part should be a crotchet, not a quaver.
[17] Note also that the chorus of cantata 145 is by Telemann, and (Note [18]) that cantata 194 was written for performance with a very low-pitched organ. It needs to be put down a tone or a semi-tone to be comfortable for singing.

APPENDIX C

Orchestration of the cantatas

A chorus and/or chorale is included unless otherwise stated. Abbreviations used: Fl = flute; Rec = recorder; Ob = oboe; Ob d'am = *oboe d'amore*; CA = Cor anglais (modern substitute for *Oboe da Caccia* and *Taille*); Fg = bassoon; Tpt = trumpet; Timp = timpani; Trb = trombone; Str = violin I, violin II, viola, violoncello, double bass (or violone); Vln = violin; Va = viola; Vcl = violoncello; Org = organ; dbl = doubling. Opening capital letters indicate soloists required; organ continuo is understood for all church works; harpsichord for secular ones.

N.B. A bassoon is implied at most times; certainly when upper wind instruments are present. It is only indicated below when it is *obbligato* or *specifically* indicated. The frequent inclusion of one horn (or *cornetto*) in the orchestration given below calls for comment: in the vast majority of cases this instrument is simply used to double the chorale melody with the sopranos in an opening chorale fantasia and closing plain chorale. Bach's sopranos may have been weak, and his congregation needed to hear the melody clearly. The range of these parts can be too high for an ordinary horn, in which case a trumpet or cornet will do. Or it can often be omitted altogether without serious loss.

Cantata

1	STB, 2 horns, 2 CA, str (includes 2 solo vln).
2	ATB, 2 ob, 3 trb, str.
3	SATB, 2 ob d'am, 1 horn, 1 trb, str.
4	SATB (but can be fully choral), *cornetto* (or tpt), 3 trb, str. (including 2 va).
5	SATB, 2 ob, tpt, str.
6	SATB, 2 ob, 1 CA, vcl piccolo, str. (soprano only sings chorale, which is better sung full or as semichorus).
7	ATB, 2 ob d'am, str. (includes 2 solo vln).
8	SATB, fl, 2 ob d'am, horn, str.
9	SATB, fl, ob d'am, str.
10	SATB, 2 ob, tpt, str.
11	SATB, 2 fl, 2 ob, 3 tpt, timp, str.
12	ATB, ob, fg, tpt, str.
13	SATB, 2 rec, CA, solo vln, str.
14	STB, 2 ob, horn, str.
16*	ATB, 2 ob (one dbl CA), horn, str.
17	SATB, 2 ob, str.
18	STB, 2 rec, fg, 4 va, vcl and bass continuo.
19	STB, 2 ob (dbl ob d'am), CA, 3 tpt, timp, str.

*Cantata 15 is not by Bach.

65

20	ATB, 3 ob, tpt, str.
21	S(A) TB, ob, fg, 3 tpt, 4 trb, timp, str.
22	ATB, ob, str.
23	SAT, 2 ob, *cornetto* (tpt), 3 trb, str.
24	ATB, 2 ob (dbl ob d'am), *clarino* (tpt), str.
25	STB, 3 rec, 2 ob, *cornetto* (tpt), 3 trb, str.
26	SATB, fl, 3 ob, horn, str.
27	SATB, 2 ob (1 dbl CA), horn, str, org *obbligato*.
28	SATB, 2 ob, CA, *cornetto* (tpt), 3 trb, str.
29	SATB, 2 ob, 3 tpt, timp, solo org, str.
30	SATB, 2 fl, 2 ob (1 dbl ob d'am), str.
	(The three trumpets and timpani given in BG are unauthentic.)
31	STB, 3 ob, CA, fg, 3 tpt, timp. str. (incl. 2 Va and 2 vcl)
32	SB, ob, str.
33	ATB, 2 ob, str.
34	ATB, 2 fl, 2 ob, 3 tpt, timp, str.
35	A, 2 ob, CA, solo org, str; no chorus or chorale.
36	SATB, 2 ob d'am, str.
37	SATB, 2 ob d'am, str.
38	SATB, 2 ob, 4 trb, str.
39	SAB, 2 rec, 2 ob, str.
40	ATB, 2 ob, 2 horns, str.
41	SATB, 3 ob, 3 tpt, timp, vcl piccolo, str.
42	SATB, 2 ob, fg, str.
43	SATB, 2 ob, 3 tpt, timp, str.
44	SATB, 2 ob, fg, str.
45	ATB, fl, 2 ob, str.
46	ATB, 2 rec, 2 CA, tpt (or horn), str.
47	SB, 2 ob, solo org, str.
48	AT, 2 ob, tpt, str.
49	SB, ob d'am, vcl piccolo, solo org, str; no chorus or chorale.
50	Single movement: only double SATB choir, 3 ob★, 3 tpt, timp. str.
51	S, tpt, str; no chorus or chorale
52	S, 3 ob, fg, 2 horns, str.
54★	A, str. (incl. 2 va)
55	T, fl, ob d'am, str.
56	B, 2 ob, CA, str.
57	SB, 2 ob, CA, str.
58	SB, 2 ob, CA, str.
59	SB, 2 tpt, timp, str.
60	ATB, 2 ob d'am, horn, str.
61	STB, fg, str. (incl. 2 va)
62	SATB, 2 ob, horn, str.
63	SATB, 3 ob, fg, 4 tpt, timp, str.
64	SAB, ob d'am, *cornetto* (or tpt), 3 trb, str.
65	TB, 2 rec, 2 CA, 2 horns, str.

★Oboe no 3 going below B♭ needs to be a d'amore or cor anglais
†Cantata 53 is not by Bach.

66	ATB, 2 ob, fg, str.
67	ATB, fl, 2 ob d'am, horn, str.
68	SB, 2 ob, CA, horn, *cornetto* (or tpt), 3 trb, str.
69	SATB, 3 ob (1 dbl ob d'am), fg, 3 tpt, timp, str.
70	SATB, ob, fg, tpt, str.
71	SATB, 2 rec, 2 ob, fg, 3 tpt, timp, str.
72	SAB, 2 ob, str.
73	STB, 2 ob, horn or *obbligato* org, str.
74	SATB, 2 ob, CA, 3 tpt, timp, str.
75	SATB, 2 ob (1 dbl d'am), tpt, str.
76	SATB, 2 ob (1 dbl ob d'am), tpt, va da gamba, str.
77	SATB, 2 ob, tpt, str.
78	SATB, fl, 2 ob, horn, str.
79	SAB, 2 fl, 2 ob, 2 horns, timp, str.
80	SATB, 2 ob (dbl ob d'am), CA, str.
	(The three trumpets and timpani given in BG were added later by W. F. Bach.)
81	ATB, 2 rec, 2 ob d'am, str.
82	B, ob, str; no chorus or chorale.
83	ATB, 2 ob, 2 horns, str.
84	S, ob, str.
85	SATB, 2 ob, str.
86	SATB, 2 ob, str.
87	ATB, 2 ob (1 dbl CA), CA, str.
88	SATB, 2 ob d'am, CA, str.
89	SAB, 2 ob, horn, str.
90	ATB, tpt, str.
91	SATB, 3 ob, 2 horns, timp, str.
92	SATB, 2 ob d'am, str.
93	SATB, 2 ob, str.
94	SATB, fl, 2 ob (1 dbl ob d'am), str.
95	STB, 2 ob (dbl ob d'am), horn (*cornettino*), str.
96	SATB, fl, high rec, 2 ob, horn, trb, vln piccolo, str.
97	SATB, 2 ob, fg, str.
98	SATB, 2 ob, CA, str.
99	SATB, fl, ob d'am, horn, str.
100	SATB, fl, ob d'am, 2 horns, timp, str.
101	SATB, fl, 2 ob, CA, *cornetto* (tpt), 3 trb, str.
102	ATB, fl, 2 ob, Vln piccolo (optional), str.
103	AT, fl (dbl piccolo (rec)), 2 ob d'am, tpt, str.
104	TB, 2 ob (dbl ob d'am), CA, str.
105	SATB, 2 ob, horn, str.
106	ATB, 2 rec, 2 va da gamba, vcl and bass continuo
107	STB, 2 fl, 2 ob d'am, horn, str.
108	ATB, 2 ob d'am, str.
109	AT, 2 ob, horn, str.
110	SATB, 2 fl, 3 ob (1 dbl ob d'am, 1 dbl CA), fg, 3 tpt, timp, str.
111	SATB, 2 ob, str.
112	SATB, 2 ob d'am, 2 horns, str.

113	SATB, fl, 2 ob (dbl ob d'am), str.
114	SATB, fl, 2 ob, horn, str.
115	SATB, fl, ob d'am, horn, vcl piccolo, str.
116	SATB, 2 ob d'am, horn, str.
117	ATB, 2 fl, 2 ob (dbl ob d'am), str.
118	Single movement: only SATB choir

  { Version 1: 2 litui, cornetto (tpt), 3 trb.
  { Version 2: 2 litui, str; [optional:– 2 ob, CA, fg].
  Substitutes for the obsolete *litui* (?horns) can be oboes and/or
  clarinets or piccolo trumpets.

119	SATB, 2 rec, 3 ob (2 dbl CA), 4 tpt, timp, str.
120	SATB, 2 ob d'am, 3 tpt, timp, str.
121	SATB, ob d'am, cornetto (tpt), 3 trb, str.
122	SATB, 3 rec, 2 ob, CA, str.
123	ATB, 2 fl, 2 ob d'am, str.
124	SATB, ob d'am, horn, str.
125	ATB, fl, ob (dbl ob d'am), horn, str.
126	ATB, 2 ob, tpt, str.
127	STB, 2 rec, 2 ob, tpt, str.
128	ATB, 2 ob (1 dbl ob d'am?), CA, 2 horns, tpt, str.
129	SAB, fl, 2 ob, 3 tpt, timp, str.
130	SATB, fl, 3 ob, 3 tpt, timp, str.
131	S (chorale only), A (chorale only), TB, ob, fg, str (vlns in unison, 2 va, vcl, bass).
132	SATB, ob, fg, str; no chorus or chorale.
133	SATB, 2 ob d'am, *cornetto* (horn or tpt), str.
134	AT, 2 ob, str.
135	ATB, 2 ob, *cornetto* (horn or tpt), trb, str.
136	ATB, 2 ob d'am (1 dbl ob), horn, str.
137	SATB, 2 ob, 3 tpt, timp, str.
138	ATB, 2 ob d'am, str.
139	SATB, 2 ob d'am, str.
140	STB, 2 ob, CA, horn, vln piccolo, str.
141	(incomplete) ATB, 2 ob, str.
143*	STB, fg, 3 horns, timp, str.
144	SAT, ob d'am, str.
145	STB, fl, 2 ob d'am, tpt, str.
146	SATB, fl, 2 ob (dbl ob d'am), CA, solo org, str.
147	SATB, 2 ob (1 dbl ob d'am, both dbl CA†), tpt, str.
148	AT, 3 ob, tpt, str.
149	SATB, 3 ob, fg, 3 tpt, timp, str.
150	SATB (but can be fully choral), fg str (no va).
151	SATB, fl, ob d'am, str.
152	SB, rec, ob d'am, va d'amore, va da gamba, vcl and bass continuo; no chorus or chorale.

*Cantata 142 is not by Bach.
†It is asking a lot to expect oboists to double on *two* instruments; one extra player (on CA) would be better.

153	ATB, str.
154	ATB, 2 ob (dbl ob d'am), str.
155	SATB, fg, str.
156	ATB, fg, str.
157	TB, fl, ob (dbl ob d'am), str.
158	S (chorale only), B, ob, solo vln, vcl and bass continuo.
159	ATB, ob, str.
161*	AT, 2 rec, str.
162	SATB, horn (or tpt), fg, str.
163	SATB, ob d'am, str. (incl. 2 vcl and continuo)
164	SATB, 2 fl, 2 ob, str.
165	SATB, fg, str.
166	ATB, ob, str.
167	SATB, ob (dbl CA), *clarino* (tpt), str.
168	SATB, 2 ob d'am, str.
169	A, 2 ob, CA, solo org, str.
170	A, ob d'am, solo org, str; no chorus or chorale.
171	SATB, 2 ob, 3 tpt, timp, str.
172	SATB, fg, 3 tpt, timp, optional solo org, str.
173	SATB, 2 fl, str.
174	ATB, 2 ob, CA, fg, 2 horns, vln I, vln II, vln III, va I, va II, va III, vcl I, vcl II, vcl III, bass continuo with fg.
175	ATB, 3 rec, 2 tpt, vcl piccolo, str.
176	SAB, 2 ob, CA, str.
177	SAT, 2 ob, CA, fg, solo vln, str.
178	ATB, 2 ob (dbl ob d'am), horn, str.
179	STB, 2 ob (dbl CA), str.
180	SATB, fl, 2 rec, 2 CA, vcl piccolo, str.
181	SATB, fl, ob, tpt, str.
182	ATB, rec, solo vln, vln I, va I, va II, vcl I, vcl II, bass.
183	SATB, ob d'am, 2 CA, vcl piccolo, str.
184	SAT, 2 fl, str.
185	SATB, ob, fg, tpt, str.
186	SATB, 2 ob, CA, str.
187	SAB, 2 ob, str.
188	SATB, ob, solo org, str.
190*	incomplete† ATB, 3 ob (1 dbl ob d'am), 3 tpt, timp, str.
191	ST, 2 fl, 2 ob, 3 tpt, timp, str.
192	incomplete; SB, 2 fl, 2 ob, str.
193	incomplete†; SA, 2 ob (1 dbl ob d'am), 3 tpt, timp, str.
194	STB, 3 ob, str.
195	SATB (as a concertante chorus I group; *solos* only for SB), 2 fl, 2 ob (dbl ob d'am), 2 horns, 3 tpt, timp, str.
196	STB, str.
197	SAB, 2 ob (dbl ob d'am), fg, 3 tpt, timp, str.

*Cantatas 160 and 189 are not by Bach.
†Reconstructions have been made by the author for the BBC; they are in the Corporation's Music Library.

198	SAT, 2 fl, 2 ob (dbl ob d'am), 2 va da gambas, 2 lutes, str.
199	S, ob, str; no chorus or chorale.
200	(single movement) A, vln I, vln II, vcl and bass continuo; no chorus or chorale.
201	SATTBB, 2 fl, 2 ob (1 dbl ob d'am), 3 tpt, timp, str.
202	S, ob, str; no chorus or chorale.
203	B, solo harpsichord; no chorus or chorale.
204	S, fl, 2 ob, str; no chorus or chorale.
205	SATB, 2 fl, 2 ob (1 dbl ob d'am), 2 horns, 3 tpt, timp, va d'amore, va da gamba, str.
206	SATB, 3 fl, 3 ob (dbl ob d'am), 3 tpt, timp, str.
207	SATB, 2 fl, 2 ob d'am, CA, 3 tpt, timp, str.
208	SSTB, 2 rec, 2 ob, CA, fg, 2 horns, str.
209	S. fl, str; no chorus or chorale.
210	S, fl, ob d'am, str.
211	STB, fl, str. } no chorus or chorale
212	SB, fl, horn, str.
213	SATB, 2 ob (1 dbl ob d'am), 2 horns, str.
214	SATB, 2 fl, 2 ob, 3 tpt, timp, str.
215	STB, Double Choir, 2 fl, 2 ob (dbl ob d'am), 3 tpt, timp, str.
217*	SATB, fl, str.
218	SATB, 2 horns, str.
219	SAB, 2 tpt, str.
220	ATB, fl, 2 ob, str.
221	TB, fg, solo org, str; no chorus or chorale.
222	incomplete; SAB, str.

*Cantata 216 is extant only in respect of the text and two of the vocal parts.

POSTSCRIPT

Since completing the main text of this book I have heard many performances and recordings of musical settings of religious texts in which the conductors give the impression of having little sympathy with the meaning of them. A recent recording of Bach's cantata 95 and a broadcast performance of Handel's Messiah spring to mind. I am aware that I could be quite wrong, and admit that everyone is entitled to his or her own viewpoint about any work of art. I feel, however, that it is worth expanding a little on what has been written in Chapter 3(b) by pointing out that it is unprofessional not to identify oneself with the spirit and/or meaning of any piece of music which one is performing, be its subject mythological (for example, Wagner or Purcell) or Christian (for example, Bach). If one does not have to 'suspend disbelief' in the latter case, so much the easier, but identify one must.